RE-ENCOUNTERS IN

Harold R. Isaacs

RE-ENCOUNTERS IN CHINA

CHINA

Notes of a Journey in a Time Capsule

An East Gate Book

M. E. Sharpe, Inc.
Armonk, New York/London

East Gate Books are edited by Douglas Merwin,
120 Buena Vista Drive, White Plains, New York 10603

Available in the United Kingdom and Europe from M. E. Sharpe,
Publishers, 3 Henrietta Street, London WC2E 8LU.

Library of Congress Cataloging in Publication Data

Isaacs, Harold Robert, 1910-
　　Re-encounters in China.

　　1. China—Politics and government—1949-
2. Authors, Chinese—20th century—Interviews.
I. Title.
DS777.75.I75　1984　　　　　951.05　　　　　84-14064
ISBN 0-87332-289-4

Printed in the United States of America

The most painful thing in life is to wake up from a dream and find no way out. Dreamers are fortunate people. If no way out can be found, the important thing is not to wake the sleepers.

Lu Hsun

CONTENTS

Preface   ix

Time Capsule in Shanghai   3

Soong Ching-ling   60

Ting Ling   76

Mao Tun   87

Liu Tsun-chi   95

About Lu Hsun   111

Chen Han-seng   118

The Doctored Photo   125

Wang Hsin-ti   142

Wu Chiang   147

Chen Yi   151

Of the Larger Politics   155

Canton   182

A Note on Some Readings   187

Romanizations   189

PREFACE

This is an account of a journey of re-encounter my wife Viola and I made to China in October 1980 at the invitation of the Chinese Writers Association and of the late Soong Ching-ling. To explain how this journey came to be made and what the re-encounters were all about, I found that my report had to become also part memoir.

Some of the small number of old friends we met again we had not seen since the war years in the 1940s, the others not since we lived and worked in Shanghai and Peking in the early 1930s. Almost all were young Communists then and most, because of the nature of my connection with them—I published a small newspaper friendly to their cause—were writers, journalists, editors, some already well known even at that time, like Mao Tun and Ting Ling, others destined to go on to play notable roles and reach high places in the Communist Party and government hierarchies in the years to come. We met them again now, men and women in their seventies and eighties. Most of them, indeed just about everyone we met, old friends or not, were newly returned from years in the limbos of Mao Tse-tung's "Cultural Revolution" of 1966-1976, and the "Anti-Rightist Campaign" that began in 1957. They were survivors of labor farms, prisons, places of exile, where several had spent as much as twenty-one years, or were newly emerged from years of house arrest or other confinement, years of isolation and silence. I report here what they had to tell us about what happened to them and to their revolution. In the short time we had, just two weeks, we could see only a few, but because of who they were and because their fates had been shared by so many thousands of fellow-victims, their accounts become a contribution to the history of the experience of these years in Mao's China.

My personal connection with these individuals during a brief but intense time I shared with them fifty years ago gave these conversations special qualities of candor, force, and feeling. It made them a complicated happening, both for those I was listening to and for me. In these pages I have tried to convey what I could of this circle-closing experience not only as they knew it in its turbulent center but also as it touched me at its outer margins.

The account is given in day-to-day diary form, all quotations and many impressions taken directly from notebooks filled as each day passed, with additional reflections and descriptions, and of course the personal material, added when the writing was done. The time element in this work is held to the time the journey took place in October 1980. Some relevant later information was added to several entries as postscripts, such as the notes on the deaths of Soong Ching-ling and Mao Tun in 1981, and several other similarly pertinent items, also in 1981, only a note or two dating more recently than that. I stress this point about the timing of this work to be clear about its nature. It is a report about some encounters with certain people in China in the fall of 1980 and my relation to them.

What I describe here is obviously dominated by China's large affairs, its politics, its crises of leadership and direction, and it is strongly colored by how these matters stood at that particular moment of this history. But these are not in themselves the subject of this book. They serve rather as the backdrop and the setting of what I did learn about a number of individuals whose whole existence had been shaped by their lifetime involvement in this larger history, whom I had first met when they were young and met again now as their own time was coming to an end. This is an account that glimpses these individual experiences, theirs, and by fleeting connection, mine. I am only too aware of how brief and limited these vignettes are, but unless and until some of these survivors do finally write their own stories about themselves and their generation, such glimpses are all we will have.

An appendix deals with the matter of romanization of Chinese names, places, and expressions. The Communist regime has adopted a new system of romanization called *pinyin* ("spelling according to sound") to replace the Wade-Giles system devised in the last century for rendering Chinese into English. (Other European languages used other systems or non-systems of their own.) Both Wade-Giles and *pinyin* do some violence to the one language or the other. Some Wade-Giles renderings produce sounds in English unrecognizable as Chinese even by speakers of the northern Chinese speech to which the system applied. Those who devised *pinyin* similarly made some arbitrary decisions about the sounds of some English letters that make many of its renderings quite unpronounceable by any English-speaker who does not know the code. For reasons of greater familiarity and easier use by readers of English, I have kept to the modified Wade-Giles or other common usage of the pre-*pinyin* time. In this matter I have followed the recent practice of supplying as an appendix a table listing the personal and place names as used in this book and in their *pinyin* equivalents, prepared with the greatly appreciated help of Ai-li Chin and some additional assistance by Donald Klein. In the text there are one or two examples where both styles occur, e.g., where I have retained in quotations the usage of "Beijing"—which is the way "Peking" always sounded when Chinese spoke it in either language—while otherwise generally rendering it as "Peking."

I acknowledge with grateful thanks the hospitality and courtesy shown to us by the Chinese Writers Association, especially our particular hosts and helpers, Li Shin and Ho Pin, and their fellow-hosts in Peking, Shanghai, and Canton. I have to thank the late Soong Ching-ling, who was responsible for the invitation that was extended to us to make this journey, and can only wish she could have read what I have written here about it, and about her.

I have profited from the friendly help and comments of Merle Goldman, Lucian and Mary Pye, John Fairbank, Irene Eber, and James Thomson, and from a particularly useful close reading of the manuscript by Arnold Isaacs. I have also benefited from readings by Irving Howe, who reproduced parts of it in his journal *Dissent,* Margaret Hollenbach, who took on at the publisher's instance the task of electronically typesetting it, and by Alexandra Goldman, Mark Smith, Deirdre Bonifaz, Jeanne Mintz, David and Debby Shipler, and Kathy Isaacs. I owe Ai-li Chin and, indirectly, Eugene Wu of the Harvard-Yenching Library, special thanks for their roles in the small chain of happenings that led to this experience of re-encounter.

Not only for help in the writing but for all aspects of what appears in this work, my chief acknowledgement belongs to Viola Robinson Isaacs, sharer of it all. This being the most personal writing I have ever done or am likely to do for print, I allow myself a further word on this subject. In the preface to my first book, *The Tragedy of the Chinese Revolution,* published in 1938, I said my thanks to "Viola Robinson, who pulled out all the weeds." This duly turned up, put to punishingly good use by an unfriendly reviewer in a British journal. It taught me to be more careful, in prefaces to all the books I have written since, to say in effect that she had pulled up all the weeds she could, and that the many that remained usually did so at my insistence that they were not weeds at all but blooms. Weeds and blooms, we have shared them all, in all the inquiring, all the working, traveling, writing, family-raising, all the living of these years. We did it all together, all but the first year and a half I was in Shanghai alone. In the course of looking over some old files during the writing of this book, I have found some of the letters I wrote to her during that interval. As a simple matter of self-protective autobiographic bias, I have made no use of them here, for they could have led the reader to wonder, as I did when I re-read them, why she ever came to join me in Shanghai in that summer of 1932. Luckily for me, she did, in her marvelous, life-giving, stubborn way, persisting in it from way back then until now. Here again, in still another preface, I thank her and congratulate myself for my great good fortune.

It is with some of the earlier details of this part of our shared experience that I hope most, through this book, to inform a certain small group of readers, Ronny, Kathy, Jenny, Katy, and Robert Isaacs, and Debby, David, Jonathan, Laura, and Michael Shipler, to whom this work is dedicated.

Newton, Massachusetts   Harold R. Isaacs
February 10, 1984

RE-ENCOUNTERS IN
CHINA

Grave marker, Martyrs Cemetery

TIME
CAPSULE
IN
SHANGHAI

Huddling under an umbrella in a chilly rain on a darkening afternoon, we stood before a stone marker in the Cemetery of the Martyrs in Lunghua, at the southern end of Shanghai. It was one of
about a hundred such heavy mottled reddish brown stones standing in even rows. Under them, we were told, lay about one thousand martyrs of the revolution buried in mass graves. A single high
shaft of plain gray stone rose at one side, overlooking the field of
the dead. From the outside, but for this shaft, the place was all but
invisible from the road going by it in this shabby far-off corner of
the great city.

Those buried here, said the official in charge, were mostly
soldier dead, killed during the final advance on the city by Mao's
Liberation Army in 1949, with the addition of some who had died
earlier fighting the Japanese. These remains were all brought here
from the older Hungjao Cemetery when this new park was made
ready in 1959. There were scattered others, he added vaguely,
buried here since then. But none, it appeared, dated further back
than the remains of the twenty-four bodies buried under the stone
before which we stood. This was the grave of the much-chronicled
"Five Martyred Writers" and the long anonymous "nineteen
others" executed at Chiang Kai-shek's Shanghai-Woosung Garrison Headquarters, not far from this spot, on the night of
February 7, 1931. After the Communist victory, their remains had
been dug up out of the grounds of the headquarters compound,
moved first to a temporary grave elsewhere in the city and finally
to this place. Only then did most of the anonymous "others"
regain the identities that had lain so long buried with their bones.
The stone before us bore photographs not only of the famous Five

but of seven others, and the names of seven more for whom pictures could not be found, leaving only five to be listed still as "unknown."

I stood there in the downpour, swept by a great jumble of feelings of waste and failure and anger and irony and sadness and loss coming out of the killing of the dreams of these young people and the killing of my own, mingled in half-shredded memories and the crowded overlay of nearly fifty years covering what had happened to them, and to me, in Shanghai so long ago. They were long gone, but here I was, on a journey of re-encounter, invited by the Chinese Writers Association to re-connect with some of that past, to meet some of its survivors, and here, at this place, to remember its dead.

*   *   *

I had come to stand at this spot because the story of these Five and the "nineteen others" had a vivid part in the shaping of my own life. I had never met them. They were arrested and executed only a few weeks after I arrived in Shanghai in early December 1930, a twenty-year-old tyro journalist in search of experience and definition, with only the dimmest flickers of political ideas in my head. I had studied something of the history of modern China, the century-long record of Western and Japanese encroachment on its sovereignty, the wars waged to control its territory, trade, and wealth, the revolutions that tried to wrench it from its desiccated past and suffocating present. Indeed, learning these things was part of what had drawn me to make my way to China as soon as I finished at Columbia College; it had taken me nearly a year, with stops to work in Honolulu and the Philippines, to get there. But I knew nothing real about the degrading life and oppressive politics of the scene into which I had come. I found work as a reporter, first with the American-owned *Shanghai Evening Post & Mercury,* and then, as an editor, with the *China Press,* newly acquired by a Chinese syndicate from its previous American owners. In these jobs, I began to learn the who-was-who and the what-was-what in this treaty port center of Western power and influence in China. The master race foreigners—British, French, American, Japanese—with their special preserves and their arrogantly held privileges dominated the subordinated and subjected Chinese in all their varieties of second-placeness, from the unbelievably rich in their great mansions down to the burden-carriers, the maimed and bleeding and whining beggars, the child prostitutes and abandoned infant dead in the streets.

The Shanghai of the early 1930s was very much the creature of its peculiar history, with its foreign-ruled enclaves created by treaties imposed nearly ninety years before, the International Settlement* and French Concession, and the sprawling Chinese city that grew up around all the licit and illicit sources of work and wealth that they provided. Treaty-protected foreigners enjoyed extraterritorial "rights"—independent political status in the country, exemption from Chinese legal jurisdiction and taxation—and the advantage of a five percent limit on China's power to tax the imports that entered the country through these treaty port establishments. These places, rights, and privileges were guarded by the foreign powers with fleets of warships and garrisons that were speedily enlarged in times of trouble (as in 1927 when the British Concession at Hankow was over-run and Shanghai seemed threatened in the same way) and with their own police forces and courts to maintain their own rule and control over their own space.

The Chinese who lived in and around these foreign enclaves were in effect a colonial population, the "natives" of a regime complete with all the trappings of the European colonial system, including the discriminations, exclusions, and racial attitudes practiced by the foreign masters and the submissive acceptance of the "treaty-port mentality" by great numbers of Chinese in their role as subjects. For many, shame and anger remained near the surface of this acceptance. It was the older more deeply rooted Chinese chauvinistic pride more than anything else that fueled the nationalist revolution that challenged this state of affairs in the 1920s. Even when he had blunted that revolution when he seized power in a coup in 1927 and began massacring his Communist allies, Chiang Kai-shek had to keep pressing the nationalist demand for abrogation of the "unequal treaties" and rendition of the foreign concessions. This was a demand, incidentally, to which his foreign friends and mentors did not yield until long after they had been deprived of their "rights" and driven from the treaty ports by

---

*Separate British and American settlements established by the treaties of 1842 were merged into the International Settlement in 1863.

their rivals, the upstart imperialist Japanese. The United States did not sign a new treaty relinquishing extraterritoriality—its first ever "equal" treaty with China—until 1943.

Society in Shanghai in the early 1930s was made up of the familiar colonial pieces: foreigners of the treaty powers, a privileged caste; an upper class of treaty port Chinese grown wealthy as participants, adjuncts, agents—"compradore" was the China coast word—of foreign enterprise, and more limitedly as aspiring competitors; a large class of Chinese white collar employees and workers making their living in both foreign and Chinese establishments; and a great mass of helot-like poor that kept flocking in from the ravaged and impoverished countryside, providing an endless supply of the laborers, human beasts of burden, beggars, prostitutes, criminals, and ultimately helpless people who left some 50,000 dead babies on the streets of the city each year—there was a philanthropic organization whose sole activity consisted of picking up and disposing of these tiny corpses. Greater Shanghai in 1930 was a city of more than three million with about 50,000 foreigners, half of them Japanese.

The French Concession existed largely as a base for the operations of the criminal gangs rooted in the old network of Yangtze Valley secret societies. They controlled the opium smuggling, gambling, prostitution, and assorted other rackets which were such a large part of the life of the city. By 1927, these gangs had come to play a cardinal political role, serving as agents of the Kuomintang in dealing with unions, radicals, and other opponents of the regime. Their principal leader, Tu Yueh-sheng, was treated with deference by both the Kuomintang and foreign authorities and was invariably referred to in the Chinese and foreign press as "a prominent merchant" and "philanthropist." These were the elements that provided much of the atmosphere and incident of the Shanghai of Malraux's *La Condition Humaine*, a novel built, with remarkable fidelity to the main facts, around the events of Chiang Kai-shek's coup in Shanghai in 1927.

In the British-dominated International Settlement (Americans, Japanese, and some token Chinese also sat on the Municipal Council), a characteristically more elaborate structure of formal legality was maintained to support the idea that the Settlement was a rock-like island of Anglo-Saxon justice in the chaotic sea of Chinese lawlessness that swirled around it. As such, the Settlement had provided asylum over the years for varieties of political "outs," especially those in whose survival foreigners had an interest or by whom they did not feel threatened. Faction-fighting warlords and politicians of high and low order were safe inside the foreign boundary. In the 1930s, Shanghai was full of such refugees from the conflict of cliques and persons in and around the newly established regime of Chiang Kai-shek. In its Shanghai version, the British "rule of law" could be stripped down to its barest pretenses and still provide some cover, some limited freedom of movement, and even of publication, for opponents of the regime. What was dangerously "illegal" outside could be at least "semilegal" or even "legal" inside the Settlement boundaries.

Where real or alleged Communists were concerned, however, these margins of difference narrowed and all but disappeared. From 1927 on, the task of ferreting out and disposing of these more dangerous enemies became a shared concern of the foreign and Kuomintang authorities. The Shanghai Municipal Police had its own "Special Branch" to deal with political matters and, like the Kuomintang, it recruited defectors and informers from among the Communists. The legal system was readily bent to these special needs. Extradition of Chinese criminals from the Settlement to Chinese jurisdiction required proceedings in a Settlement court to establish that there was a "prima facie" case against them. This was done with due care when the accused had done nothing worse than steal or kill; it became a swift and farcical procedure when it involved individuals arrested as "Communists." Between 1930 and 1932, Settlement courts handed over 326 real or alleged Communists to the Kuomintang, the prima facie case frequently consisting of the production of a piece of "Communist literature," often a simple anti-Japanese leaflet. No one ever knew how many of these disappeared into Kuomintang prisons or, like the Five Writers and those nineteen others arrested that January night in 1931, went to their deaths at the hands of Kuomintang executioners waiting just beyond the Settlement limits.

My grasp of these matters came in stages. What I saw first was a scene dominated by the brutally unequal relationship between "foreigner" and "Chinese." It took a little more time for me to bring into focus more of what lay also between "Chinese" and "Chinese." The week the Five Writers and the nineteen others were executed, I was just beginning my brief tenure as one of the editors of the *China Press* under its new Chinese owners. It was to be the first Chinese-owned English-language daily ever published in the city. I took a grandly naive view of the opportunity. "A new path is to be blazed," I wrote in an exuberant front page editorial. "We hope to give our readers a clear and coherent and accurate picture of China today." Unlike the blinkered foreign press, we would offer our readers the fruits "of intellectual honesty and newsgathering efficiency." Hitherto, the English-reading public was "handicapped in its judgment for lack of facts. Our columns shall offer the solution." I also wrote a full page advertisement that we ran in other newspapers the same day, proclaiming in heavy black type: "The new *China Press* aims to fill a hole that has been empty since the first foreigner stepped ashore on Chinese soil."

Well, it did not take long for this experience to run its course. I quickly learned what gyrations it took to help edit a daily in Shanghai for a Chinese syndicate that also owned several Chinese-language dailies, was subject to the pressures of the Kuomintang government in Nanking, and had as its managing director a man named Hollington Tong, who had once been Chiang Kai-shek's teacher and had become one of Chiang's most faithful, tense, timid, and voluble minions. He and I argued almost every night, usually over what could and could not be said in stories and headlines dealing with news from Nanking. Besides having to learn how to tread lightly on the thin ice of Chinese politics, I had to discover the game of substituting words for realities which was played one way or another every day, some days more wildly than others. The example I remember best came one day in an official Kuo Min News Agency report in its regular daily service which said that as a result of talks about modifying the system of extraterritoriality, the American and British warships had left their usual mooring places in the Whangpoo River off the Bund. I first went out to have a look, then came back and called Kuo Min's man in Shanghai whose name was Li Choy, whose head was always cocked, expression always quizzical, mouth always crooked with a sardonic smile. I told him the gray ships were still there, as he and I knew they would be. "Not according to our report," he said, and hung up.

Holly Tong and I had become friends, after our fashion. I had come even to enjoy our arguments mainly because I learned so much from them. He looked kindly on me mainly, I think, because one night I tried to dissuade him from answering a summons to go to Nanking where a factional crisis of some kind was coming to a head and I thought he might be arrested. (Years later he reminded me of that night in the midst of another argument about censorship we were having in Chungking in 1944 when he was Chiang's Minister of Information and I was a war correspondent for *Newsweek*.) When I quit the *China Press* in May 1931 after only four months, Holly accepted my resignation. A broken vase, "no matter how cleverly mended," he wrote me sadly, could never again be as it was. But he saved "face" for both of us by appointing me a roving correspondent, beginning with an announcement, featured on the front page with pictures, that I and a friend, a South African newsman named Frank Glass, were leaving for a trip up the Yangtze River.

Glass and I left Shanghai to see something of this vast country, chugging up the great river in a squat little steamer, draft shallow enough to make it almost flat-bottomed, steel-plated around the bridge for armor against rifle fire from unfriendly "bandits" on the riverbanks. Wherever we stopped to load or offload cargo at riverports—Kiukiang, Hankow, Shasi, Wanhsien, Ichang—for hours and days ashore we wandered the streets and alleys, looking, asking, taking in the glares or curious stares of people and a thousand other wordless impressions of the life around us. During the long slow days of passage against the wide river's swift current, we engaged in endless hours of talk about the world and its affairs, politics, and how one lived one's life. From the bridge our captain, a hard-seamed American named Anderson, never failed to toot salutes to passing American and other foreign gunboats, also squat and shallow-drafted craft, which patrolled the whole length of the river, periodically reassuring missionaries and businessmen in the riverports, fearful always of some Chinese trespass on their extraterritorial rights and property. We were forever passing great and small junks and sampans carrying people and goods through the vast central valley of the land. One prime item of their cargo was opium. Opium was officially contraband. At every port there was an "Opium Suppression Bureau." But opium moved in many of these boatloads, and at every port the "smugglers" stopped in at the Opium Suppression Bureaus to contribute to the opium trade tribute that made up a substantial part of Chiang Kai-shek's revenues. At the valley's end beyond Ichang where the great Yangtze Gorges began, we were pulled through the churning current by long lines of naked trackers straining at their ropes, edging slowly forward along paths cut out of the storied cliffs lining the upper reaches of the river, coming finally to Chungking, a thousand and five hundred miles inland from the sea.

From Chungking, where Glass turned back, I went on alone for weeks more, by bus, pony, and on foot, to Chengtu and beyond, deep into western Szechwan as far as Tachienlu at the beginning of the Himalayan ascent into Tibet. From that last stretch at the far end of this long journey of discovery, one encounter and two moments of sensation rise unbidden to the surface of memory. The encounter was with a young American missionary couple with whom I stayed as a paying guest in their comfortable western-style house inside of the compound of the major missionary institution in this part of the country, West China Union University, in Chengtu. In a conversation that must have begun with some aggressive questioning by me, I discovered that they were deeply troubled by what they had come to see as the intolerable contradictions of the missionary enterprise and their own role in it. They were close to deciding to leave, or were at least facing their dilemma with great pain. I do not know what choice they made, but I remember gratefully that they taught me one of my early lessons about what I eventually came to call "witless generalizations" about the varieties of human experience.

The first of the two moments of sensation was the fragrance of *kwei-hua,* a thickly growing golden bloom, that reached me one day on the road west of Chengtu, rising from gardens ahead of me planted long ago by some royal or ducal master of this land, carried in the air for miles by the western breeze, drawing the traveler on like a character in an ancient tale toward some ineffable enchantment. The second was the sight of the great mountains rising from the western Szechwan plain, so close and clear from where I looked up at them from a spot near the foot of the steep road leading up the slopes from Tachienlu. There was an open market there by the road where mountain people, so different in face, figure, dress, and speech, came down to exchange wares with the lowland Chinese. From one of them I bought the two Tibetan *tankas,* temple hangings, old and stunning, that still hang on our walls. I came there day after day and finally had to wrench myself away, fighting off the impulse to keep on going up that road into those mountains and on to the top of the world that lay beyond them.

There were sights and beauties enough along the whole way I had come, enough to teach me how to look ever after at Chinese painting, but never enough to offset for more than a relieving moment the daily exposure to what one never saw in Chinese painting, namely people, masses of human beings trapped in toil and poverty and disease. Not all the fragrance of all the *kwei-hua* in China could cover the stench and filth that pervaded so many places through which I could walk like a visitor from another planet, not subject to any of their pains and rigors as, indeed, being an extraterritorial foreigner, I was not subject to their laws. I had only to hold my nose against the smell for a few hours at a time. And as though chance itself was intent on extending this experience to extremes, having come upriver through so many scenes of ordinary hardship imposed on people by a social order, I went back downriver amid extraordinary suffering inflicted by a great natural disaster, all the deaths and unattended mass miseries of the Yangtze River flood of 1931. Floating corpses and wreckage glutted the river all the way down, my first experience of horror on such an enormous scale.

Except for pulling a few stranded refugees aboard the small boat, I traveled down the Min River back to the Yangtze at Suifu, 200 miles west of Chungking, I passed through all of this as an onlooker, helpless and unhelping. This separation of fates and involvement bore in on me hard throughout this journey across the whole breadth of the country in those months. Of foreigners I had encountered here and there I wrote at the time, sweepingly as was my wont but not too inaccurately: "Any early concern with the conditions among the Chinese soon gave way to the well known extraterritorial indifference and a complete willingness to fall in line with the great shoulder-shrugging fraternity." The lesson I was drawing turned up at the end of another article I wrote about a Chinese general in command of a district in western Szechwan, a frustrated reformer who spoke of having to trim his vision of possible change to what was "possible" without threatening his own position in the system. My own evolving feelings led me to write of his dilemma with unwonted sympathy, adding in a last sentence: "I felt too keenly myself the extent to which convictions are so often left untranslated into action.'' That article appeared, of all places, in the magazine section of the austerely British *North China Sunday News.*

In September I was in Nanking on a string assignment for the United Press to cover the arrival there of Charles Lindbergh, who had been making an aerial survey of the flood damage for the government. We were actually clustered around him for an outdoor press conference on the airfield that day, September 19, 1931, when someone brought word that the Japanese Army had begun the night before to move out of the South Manchuria Railway Zone following an explosion on the tracks near the city of Mukden which they said was an attack. They had moved with the evident intention of extending their occupation of the railway zone to the whole of Manchuria, known to the Chinese as their Northeast. We all left Lindbergh and made for the Chinese Foreign Office where we shortly heard the Foreign Minister, Wang Chengting, a suave gentleman known to everyone as C.T. Wang, announce in effect that Chiang Kai-shek's government would pursue a policy of non-resistance to the Japanese invasion, would appeal to the League of Nations while continuing to try to deal more effectively with its opponents closer to home. Even a tyro student of international power politics could see that Japan was directly challenging the established positions of British and American influence in China and, by moving northward in Manchuria, was on its way to putting its forces on the border of the Soviet Union. It took no great clairvoyance to see even then, and it can easily be seen now, that Japan's move into Manchuria in 1931 was in effect the beginning of the big history of our years, the opening of the era of the Second World War.

This turn in big events widened and luridly colored the setting in which I was making a turn of my own in the small events of my own life during those fall months in Shanghai. The larger fate involving everyone was now not just dimly seen; it had become sharply visible to me under the dazzling light of Marxist revelation about the class struggle and commanding need for revolution to resolve it on the side of the greater good for the greater number. I had seen this light on the road I traveled across China where the appalling realities of exploitation and deprivation had unrolled so vividly before my eyes. Now the clashes of great Powers and the threat of war added their enormous weight to the personal choices that lay before me. It was not just a question of how I would live my life but of how I would take part in history. It was an intense experience, arming oneself with ready answers to the riddles of human existence, making the passage from detachment to involvement, ceasing to be just a spectator and becoming an actor in the drama. Many of my age and time shared this experience. Where I happened to be, in Shanghai just then, it was a chance to play a small part in some high drama indeed.

* * *

These exposures and sensations, shocks and encounters, the learning of these crowded months, all came together for me soon enough when Communist friends and friends of Communists I met in Shanghai came up with the idea that I should start a paper of my own. I took it up with alacrity. After some casting about in odd news jobs, I had solved my livelihood problem when I was hired by the French Havas News Agency bureau to translate their French news report into English for local distribution. This took me only a few hours a day, did not engage my emotions, and paid me enough to live on, and I did it so well that my employers kept me on through all that followed. Thus I could offer myself to the cause pure in heart, make no claim on the payroll, remain untainted by gain. The subsidy I was offered would all go to the enterprise itself, a consummation much more to be desired, I thought, than becoming what I learned to call a "professional revoutionary." Instead, I kept my amateur status intact, and with it my independence, a great gift of my innocence. The result, after weeks of preparation, was the *China Forum,* which began as an eight-page tabloid size English-language weekly. The first issue appeared on January 13, 1932. Once again, I wrote a manifesto-like opening editorial, this time with the title "Stifled Voices":

> China, with the rest of a tottering world, is struggling for existence. . . . Lies, distortions, omissions, purposely or otherwise contrived, characterize the entire press of China, foreign language and Chinese, in its treatment of every phase of these struggles. The voices of those in power . . . enjoy a complete monopoly of the press. All other voices are stifled—or modulated. . . . The *China Forum* does not subscribe to the fiction of impartiality. . . . To be without bias in a world of conflict between an old order that is dying and a new one being born is to be a fool, an ignoramus, a liar—or all three. The

China Forum (is to be) a vehicle for the publication of news and opinions . . . which at present have no outlet, no way of getting their version of events into print . . . to break through this fabric of lies, distortion, and silence.

The first issue included a review of the student anti-Japanese movement that had risen in response to the government's non-resistance policy. It also featured an entire page devoted to pictures of the Five Writers and a sixth earlier victim, the story of their arrest and execution, along with the "nineteen others," and details of the international campaign of protest by writers, intellectuals, and other notables that had been generated around the case by the Communist International in America and Europe. The second issue, on January 20, included a translation of a short story by one of the five, Hu Yeh-pin, beginning a series of fourteen more stories by various writers which appeared in translation in the *Forum* during its lifetime.

There was nothing smooth about the *Forum's* path to its kind of truth-telling. The day its third issue appeared, January 28, 1932, Japanese army, naval, and air forces attacked Chinese Shanghai and met with unexpected resistance from the garrisoning Nineteenth Route Army which fought back in defiance of orders from Nanking. The battle lasted thirty-four days. It introduced the world to carpet-bombing. Chapei, the large jammed working class quarter of Shanghai adjoining the International Settlement, was systematically laid waste. We watched it happen, day after day, from the privileged sanctuary of the Settlement into which only a few bombs fell by mistake, for which the Japanese authorities punctiliously apologized. It was the world's first glimpse of what air war was to become. The purpose was sheer terror, there were no military targets in Chapei. It was a rehearsal for what lay ahead in Guernica, Coventry, Dresden, Hiroshima, Vietnam, Cambodia. Having only barely recovered from the sight of dead bodies floating in the rampaging Yangtze, I now saw bodies strewn in the streets, men, women, children, in bloody bits and pieces, victims of rampaging men. My head filled for the first time with the sound of shells, gunfire, exploding bombs, my self filled with enough of the fear, anger, and hate it took to turn me into a potentially rampaging man myself, ready to kill. I did in fact one day at an edge of the fighting around North Station, pick up a masher-style grenade

MAY, 1932   THE CHINA FORUM   15

Five Young Writers Butchered By the Kuomintang, February 7, 1931

FENG KUNG (1907-31)   HU YEH-PIN (1905-31)   JOU SHIH (1901-31)   LI WEI-SEN (1903-31)   YIN FU (1909-31)

"In Lunghua, over the mass graves in which more than 10,000 of our revolutionary dead have been buried since 1927, we will one day erect a monument of commemoration. We will carve the names of our hero dead in stone to last 10,000 years......" (Left Wing Writers League)

Five writers from *China Forum*, 1931*

and hurl it in a futile gesture toward the Japanese firing from the ruins on the far edge of the station plaza. (One day twelve years later, in an obscure corner of the much bigger war in which I was again an onlooking non-combatant correspondent, I stood on top of a hill looking down on the Salween River gorge in faraway southern Yunnan, borrowed an M-1 rifle and fired it at a Japanese position on a knob of hill a few hundred yards away. I did so with those days in Shanghai sharp and vivid and terrible in my mind.)

The first three issues of the *China Forum* were printed at a press in the French Concession. When the Japanese attack began, the Concession authorities invoked the emergency to put a ban on the paper. No press in the Settlement would take me on. When I could resume publication in March after the fighting ended, there were difficulties of other kinds, official and unofficial surveillance, some more printers frightened off, mail intercepted, bundles of the paper seized, copies "lost" at the post office, all the problems of functioning overground when so much of the enterprise had to stay underground. It was still the extraterritorial system, of course, that made it possible for the *Forum* to exist at all. The Chiang Kai-shek regime was imprisoning and killing Chinese every day for doing even less than I was doing, and by this time there were not a few foreigners and Chinese who wished it could do the same to me. Early that summer of 1932, the Nanking government filed a pro-

*These pictures appeared in the first issue of the *China Forum,* January 13, 1932, along with a sixth, of twenty-one-year-old Tsung Hui, who had been arrested and executed earlier. This set of five pictures of the February 7 victims appeared again in a special issue of the *Forum,* titled "Five Years of Kuomintang Reaction," May 1932.

test with the American authorities, including a bill of charges against me most of which called for the death penalty under Kuomintang law. I was first called in to the Consulate General and asked informally by the United States attorney, a man named George Sellett, why I did not voluntarily waive my "rights" since I thought them so reprehensible. I was not quite that naive. I was next summoned officially by the Consul General himself, one Edwin Cunningham. Flanked by the attorney and a junior consul, he read to me from Washington's reply to the protest. It said that unless I modified my paper's policy, "The United States Government would not be constrained to have any of its officers intervene" should the Chinese authorities take action against me. When I promptly made this known to the local foreign press corps, cries of alarm came from some of the most conservative spokesmen in British Shanghai, concerned not for me, certainly, but for the principle of extraterritoriality. A leading British columnist, H.G.W. Woodhead, urged deportation as a better remedy, citing precedents of accused murderers who had been sent home for trial. The hubbub reached all the way back to the *New York Times* (which headlined a column-long story on July 30, 1932: "American Editor Warned of Trial by China—Death Penalty Possible"), my father's Congressman, Fiorello La Guardia, and the State Department, which finally did indicate that it did not mean what its words had seemed to mean when they were passed to me in Shanghai.*

This high level pressure eased—the "rights" were plainly more important than my neck—but low level pressure increased and proved to be more effective. After putting through two more

*The official American version of this episode, recorded in the telegrams that passed between the Shanghai Consulate General and the State Department in Washington, appears in *Foreign Relations of the U.S., Diplomatic Papers,* 1932, Vol. IV, Government Printing Office, Washington, D.C., 1947-48, pp. 654-661. The pages immediately following, 661-669, deal with an attempt by the Nanking Government to compel foreign publications to register with the Chinese authorities or else forfeit their postal privileges. The immediate example involved was the attempted denial of postal privileges to a monthly called *Far Eastern Review,* edited by an American named George Bronson Rea, who had made it, quite undisguisedly, an organ of Japanese propaganda. Rea himself was at that time in Geneva acting as an adviser to the Japanese delegation to the League of Nations where the issue of the Japanese-created puppet state of "Manchoukuo" in Manchuria was being debated. The U.S. authorities protested the denial of postal rights to the *Far Eastern Review* and

issues of the *Forum,* nos. 23 and 24, following these official encounters, my printer, the last in the Settlement who would take me
in, was persuaded to throw me out. I had no choice but to begin
putting together a small printshop of my own. When the *China
Forum* resumed publication some months later, it appeared bilingually in English and Chinese.

It was a lively time in the very midst of which, on a hot August
day in 1932, Viola Robinson, two years out of Barnard as I was
out of Columbia, wearing a floppy white hat and a green and
white dress, stepped off a tender at the jetty on the Shanghai Bund
where I was waiting to welcome her. Her coming was the result of
the other crucial personal choice made in the time of decision these
months past, of two commitments made, mine to radical politics,
hers and mine to each other. Fortunately, especially for me, we
chose not to regard them as incompatible despite much that made
them seem so. We began together the process of learning that
while the gods of politics could and did fail, love could and did
conquer all. The day after my twenty-second birthday and only a
bit more after hers, we were married at that same American Consulate General, to the bemusement of some and the irritation of
other officials who wished I would just go away. Viola's arrival
made it less likely that I would and, indeed, as it turned out, they
had to put up with me, now us, for a year and a half more.

Besides providing these unforeseen advantages for this particular beneficiary, the extraterritorial system also had openings
through which much else did pass. The foreign-controlled areas
did provide some protective covering for some Chinese who could
stay "legal," as quite a few could, or stay successfully hidden, as
quite a few did. Chinese literary journals with only the barest

---

rejected the demand for registration as inconsistent with extraterritorial rights.
In a telegram to the U.S. Minister in Peking on October 4, 1932, the State
Department said: "Although the American Government might be prepared in
certain cases, when circumstances warrant, to acquiesce in a denial to
American nationals of postal facilities by the Chinese authorities, as for instance in the recent case of the Isaacs publication at Shanghai, the American
Government does not admit the right of the Chinese Government
generally . . . to compel [American nationals] to comply with a Chinese law
which under the extraterritorial system is not applicable to them and which
subjects them to penal provisions which the Chinese authorities have no right
to impose." (*Ibid.* pp. 664-665.) The pro-Japanese *Far Eastern Review* evidently stood well within this pale as the pro-Communist *China Forum* did not.

pretense to political innocence kept appearing, being suppressed, appearing again under other names. Non-Communist opponents of the regime carried on a considerable activity of publication and propaganda, though always within legal limits. The police were not as efficient as they wished to be, never as efficient as the equivalent Communist policing of a later day. Things went on in Shanghai under the British, the French, and the Kuomintang that would be quite inconceivable under the Communists.

Thus a fugitive Indochinese Communist leader, already famous as "Nguyen Ai Quoc" (Nguyen lover-of-his-country), later better known as Ho Chi Minh, lived underground uncaught in Shanghai for more than a year, near enough overground for me, with due conspiratorial care, to meet him often at or near the Chinese YMCA where he stayed, walking distance from police headquarters in the Settlement. He was a slight wiry man who always seemed to regard his condition of constant peril with a certain humorous detachment. After finishing a prison term in Hong Kong, he had barely escaped being handed over to the French who wanted him on heavy charges of their own. With the help of English friends, he was put on a British steamer for Shanghai where he contacted someone—I never knew who it was—who put him in touch with me, dangerously, I thought, for I feared that every time we met he was taking a much greater risk than was needful. The Party people in Shanghai were presumably minimizing the possible risk to themselves. The purpose, besides keeping him supplied with money for his modest keep, was to help him get out and on his way to Europe. This had its lessons for me too. Following the re-opening of diplomatic relations between Russia and China in 1933, Soviet freighters from Vladivostok had begun to put into Shanghai. When I naively proposed to the Tass correspondent, the only Russian I knew in Shanghai, that Ho be smuggled aboard one of these freighters when it left port, I learned something about how Russians saw their priorities. The Tass man, named Chernov, stared at me in cold reproof. Was I mad enough to think they would risk their new trade link this way? What he doubtless saw as an example of "infantile leftism," I saw as a concrete example of the working of Stalin's policy of "socialism in one country" and the priority of Russian interest above all else. It added materially to my growing store of doubts and questions about the character of the Russian regime.

An alternative was to try to get Ho a passport with which he could leave Shanghai in some more conventional fashion. At one point this involved having photos taken in which, by way of disguise, he appeared with his hair parted in the middle instead of on the side as before, an episode in which we shared some hilarious moments. Ho's escape from Shanghai took place after I left, having turned my responsibility for him back to others through the good offices, as I remember it, of Soong Ching-ling. When I met him again in Hanoi in 1945, he was president of the brand new "Democratic Republic of Viet Nam" and I was a correspondent for *Newsweek:* there was too much else to talk about to leave time for me to ask him how he finally did get away.

Soong Ching-ling, widow of the founder of the Kuomintang, Sun Yat-sen, was one of the small number of highly visible and important Chinese figures who were able to give public voice to political opposition from relatively protected positions. Another was the writer Lu Hsun whose great repute shielded him from arrest, if not from suppression of some of his work and constant harassment, including anonymous threats on his life. One of Soong Ching-ling's principal allies was the aging educator Tsai Yuan-pei, another major figure beyond reach of any ordinary attack. He was the head of Peking National University in its greatest days as a source of revolutionary ferment (1917-23), became a leading liberal member of the Kuomintang and was at this time head of the Academia Sinica in Nanking. His chief aide, Yang Chien, general secretary of the Academia Sinica, took a major part in the work of protest and exposure of Kuomintang repression that could be carried on by these individuals because of their personal prestige and under the fragile cover of Settlement legality.

One such effort was in behalf of a German couple first known as the Noulens, then as Paul and Gertrud Ruegg, charged with being Communist agents, which they were. But they had been in prison untried for about a year and it proved possible to assemble a quite impressive committee of Chinese liberals joined, quite unprecedentedly, by a number of the top American correspondents and editors in Shanghai, in an appeal that they be given a quick and fair trial. The Americans had proved ready enough, when I asked them, to add their names to a list assembled abroad that included such luminaries as Romain Rolland, Theodore Dreiser, Sinclair Lewis, Clarence Darrow, and dozens of other notables from different countries. It was the kind of mobilization in the name of social justice that the international Communist apparatus learned in those years to carry out with great skill. The Rueggs' child, five-year-old Jimmy, was under the care of a Swiss Communist lawyer, Jean Vincent, who had come to represent the Rueggs. Jimmy lived with a kindly German woman in Shanghai and at least once a month for nearly a year after she arrived, Viola took him and Frau Holz by train to Nanking and into the prison to visit his parents, along with books to read and packages of food, bringing back almost every time their angrily impatient pleas for quicker action on their behalf.

But even more directly aimed at the Nanking government itself was the China League for Civil Rights, formed by Soong Ching-ling, Tsai Yuan-pei, Lu Hsun, Yang Chien, along with Agnes Smedley and myself, which for many months in 1933 was able to carry a number of Chinese liberals in Shanghai and Peking along with it in protests against summary arrests and executions, and conditions in which political prisoners were held. Soong Ching-ling led this band a good deal further than many in it wanted to go, intervening vigorously on behalf of arrested individuals, and even leading a delegation into a Nanking prison to visit prisoners, especially a prominent Communist leader, Lo Teng-hsien, who had fallen into Settlement police hands and been extradited. I was a member of that delegation and described in the *Forum* what I saw and heard. We could not help Lo. He was executed not long afterward. Members of the Peking branch of the League, headed by the well-known intellectual Hu Shih, made a similar prison visit in that city but the group there came apart over issues generated by the more radical approach of the parent League in Shanghai.

This activity was also made more possible in part by the rise of a popular anti-Japanese movement set in motion by the initial Japanese attack and spurred by episodes of sporadic resistance to the advancing Japanese by local Chinese armies in northern Manchuria, in Shanghai, and in the southern Manchurian province of Jehol. A national anti-Japanese boycott was launched with at least nominal government approval at first, and for a time was quite widespread and successful. There were large student demonstrations demanding patriotic resistance to the invaders. New organizations sprang up on all sides, businessmen and merchants, students, factory workers, writers, and intellectuals, banding

together under the anti-Japanese banner. One of the largest and
most successful of these was the National Salvation Association—
Soong Ching-ling was one of its founders—which worked out of
a headquarters in the Settlement and had branches in all parts of
Shanghai. It carried on an intensive activity of propaganda and
demonstrations that lasted until one day in May 1933 when Settlement police, working in tandem with Chinese police in their
territory, raided and smashed the headquarters and all the branch
offices. In the Settlement office alone, 135 persons were arrested
that day.

The long-weakened Communist movement in Shanghai and
other cities made great efforts to put itself in front of this fresh
popular surge. Battered and fragmented, the Party nevertheless
could and did hold its secret meetings, and the small groups under
its auspices and its members in larger public organizations managed to carry on a semi-public semi-secret life. The Party's boldest
propaganda coup of the year in Shanghai was the holding of an
"Anti-War Congress"—anti-imperialist war, that is—that was
publicly announced and conspiratorially held right in the heart of
the city. It was actually attended by a delegation of visiting Europeans—Lord Marley of the British Labor Party, Paul Vaillant-
Couturier, editor of the French Communist daily *L'Humanite,* a
Belgian Communist named Marteau and a French socialist named
Poupy, and more than fifty Chinese delegates, including some
who came, the Party said, from all parts of the country, including
the Chinese "Red Army districts" in the mountains in far-off
Kiangsi. Soong Ching-ling opened the meeting and Lord Marley
presided. I was there, too, looking on and listening, taking notes
for the account I published, complete with documents, in the
Forum. It took many hours of comings and goings and all kinds of
evasive action to assemble and disassemble this gathering, all of it
miraculously successful in escaping surveillance. It was a pity that
all this conspiratorial virtuosity could not have been more usefully
employed. It produced a showpiece that altered none of the
realities of the situation.

In the anti-Japanese movement, the Party claimed a good deal
more for itself than the facts often justified, but it was greatly
helped when the Kuomintang authorities, moving to blunt and halt
this popular activity, began to equate "anti-Japanese" with
"Communist." This identification stood the Communists in good

stead as pressure for resistance to the Japanese grew, coming now also from some of Chiang's militarist rivals, especially those driven from the northeast by the Japanese attack. In 1934, Chiang Kai-shek's "bandit-suppression campaign" finally did compel Mao Tse-tung to lead his peasant forces on their famous "Long March" from central China to a new base in Shensi, in the far northwest, with its headquarters at Yenan. But two years later Chiang was finally brought to turn around and face the Japanese who were extending their piecemeal attacks into an all-out assault aimed at total control in all of China. The war that followed gave Mao's peasant armies the chance to come out of their distant refuge and begin moving toward their eventual victory.

In 1933, however, the skeleton Communist movement that still existed in the cities was all but shattered by hardened Kuomintang repression. Chiang Kai-shek's semi-private semi-official anti-Communist apparatus came to include the Lan I-Shang, called the Blue Jackets or Blue Shirts, or, literally, Blue Gowns, taking on some of the styles and methods of Mussolini's Blackshirts and Hitler's Brownshirts. The Nazi model was especially admired by Chiang, whose armies pursuing the Communists in central China were trained and partly staffed by German advisers. His anti-Communist gangs, rooted in the old criminal secret societies, became a highly politicized band of agents, spies, and thugs who began an aggressive drive against Chiang's opponents in the cities, especially among intellectuals. They engaged in intimidation, beatings, kidnappings, torture, and murder, invaded and smashed offending bookstores, film studios, and publishing houses. They began also to turn out more newspapers, magazines, and films of their own. Blue Jackets made "illegal" raids into the Settlement and French Concession, seizing their victims and taking them out of the foreign areas, bypassing the flimsy procedures of arrest and extradition through the Settlement and Concession systems, much to the annoyance and discomfiture of foreign officials jealous of their prerogatives.

One of the best publicized examples was the kidnapping of the young writer Ting Ling, widow of the writer Hu Yeh-pin, one of the Five executed at Lunghua. Ting Ling and a fellow writer, Pan Tze-nien, were taken from her Settlement apartment and driven away. Later that day, a third writer, the even more youthful Ying Hsu-jen, came to visit, was seized by the Kuomintang thugs

FIVE YEARS
OF
KUOMINTANG REACTION

Issued As A Special Edition
of the
Vol. I, Nos. 11-12-13 **CHINA FORUM** May, 1932

Cover of a special edition of *China Forum*, May 1932

waiting there, and when he fought back was thrown to his death in the street below. The *China Forum* was able to do full dramatic, even melodramatic justice to the event with details supplied by an informant who was apparently a double agent and was actually a member of the raiding party. From him we got the license number of the kidnap car and traced it to the Bureau of Public Safety, the police establishment of Chinese Shanghai. This heightened the attention given to the event in the foreign press since it indicated official involvement by Chinese authorities in another violation of extraterritoriality. Ting Ling, whose story about her husband's execution, called "One Certain Night," had appeared in the *Forum,* disappeared from view and for many weeks was thought to have been killed. The *Forum* did all it could to keep pressing for more information about what had happened to her.

The *Forum* reported other cases of this kind, some of them reflected in its translations of short stories by writers who were living through the experience. One such was by a young writer named Lo Shih-yi in which he described a girl caught in this way and tortured until she died. Some weeks later, Lo Shih-yi himself disappeared the same way in his turn. No one then in Shanghai could mistake the characters in such stories for creatures of the writers' imaginations. Ex-Communist defectors *were* walking the streets to spot their former comrades. Sadistic jailers, torturers, and executioners *were* operating in official and unofficial Kuomintang locations in and around Shanghai. Young people *were* fearfully resisting or ultimately yielding, dying, or somehow surviving to die another day.

It was a heavy time in Shanghai for this young crusading radical journalist caught up in baleful happenings. The *Forum* received and published a list of targeted victims drawn up by the Blue Jackets. It included the names of both radical and non-radical intellectuals and politicians who shared only their identification as opponents and critics of the Nanking regime. On June 18, 1933, only a few weeks after Ting Ling was kidnapped, one of those named on this list, Yang Chien, close collaborator with Soong Ching-ling in the China League for Civil Rights, was murdered on the street in front of his house as he and his small son were getting into a car. Inevitably after that, all who thought of themselves as opponents and critics shrank back into deeper cover and silence. Most of the handful of Chinese liberals who had been drawn into the League's activity by the appeal and prestige of Soong Ching-ling drew away from it. Yang Chien's young son survived and so, barely, did the League for Civil Rights, and for half a year more, so did the *China Forum*.

These were events in which I shared, some at first hand, others at close enough quarters. I was able to move about myself with a peculiar mix of freedom and constraint. When I saw Ting Ling again during this journey of re-encounter, she presented me with a small book of her recently published memoirs, calling my attention to a passage in which she recalled seeing me and Agnes Smedley at one of the large student anti-Japanese demonstrations. Wu Chiang, a grizzled veteran of seventy, now head of the Shanghai Branch of the Writers Association, reminded me that we had met before, at the organizing meeting of the anti-Japanese writers group in Shanghai in 1932. I got around a good deal in those days in my role as reporter for my own paper. When the Rueggs were finally given an open hearing in Nanking, partly, we liked to think, because of the pressure we generated, I went to Nanking and covered the proceedings myself, filling columns of the *Forum* with a detailed description and excerpts of nearly verbatim testimony that I recorded myself. Late in 1933, when a group of anti-Chiang politicians of various fringe opposition parties and some rival generals (including Tsai Ting-kai, the hero of the resistance at Shanghai), set up a rebel government at Foochow, capital of the southern province of Fukien, I went there by coastal steamer, interviewed them all, and returned to write a lengthy account of what turned out to be a short-lived challenge to Kuomintang rule. I even delivered some money from Communist friends in Shanghai to emissaries who came to Foochow from the "Red districts" in neighboring Kiangsi. I carried it, in blatantly storybook fashion, sewn into the lining of my coat.*

My high visibility in Shanghai was an advantage, even a safeguard of a kind, but also a severe handicap. I had to be careful

---

*I carried contraband money one other time in my career as a brusher-past of revolutions, to Indonesia in 1949 when the Dutch were conducting a euphemistically called "police action" against the Indonesian nationalists. I brought in a considerable sum of dollars curled around the inside of my portable typewriter. The previous episode in Fukien had been flagrantly subversive but this time the purpose was purely philanthropic. The money, entrusted to me by a refugee Indonesian nationalist leader in Singapore, was converted into

about Chinese seen in my company. Whenever I did meet anyone vulnerable to arrest, it was only after taking great pains to see that I was not followed to the rendezvous. At such encounters, names were rarely mentioned. I never knew who was who among the shadowy Chinese Communist figures I met occasionally. I was in touch with a succession of European Comintern representatives whom I knew only by fictitious first names. I did not even know the real names of the young Chinese who worked at such risk for the *Forum,* not even one who lived and worked sequestered in our apartment for months at a time. The conspiratorial rule was that what one did not know one could not tell. In any case, the business of this ardent young foreign sympathizer was to get out the *Forum,* to write about the outside world, the large politics, Japan, the war in China, the Powers, about the Kuomintang regime, its rule and its terror, not to learn, or really have any chance to know, what was going on in the Communist Party, its internal conflicts, or even about the tensions between Party people and writers like Lu Hsun, whom I did know and see from time to time, though never to talk about such matters as these.

Despite interruptions, sometimes for days and weeks, once for several months, the *China Forum* persisted. It kept appearing for thirty-nine issues, the last sixteen of them bilingually in Chinese and English, set by hand and printed on a small flatbed press in a tiny shop of our own on the Settlement side of the street that bordered on Chinese Chapei. Its last issue appeared on January 13, 1934, exactly two years after the first. The end came not because the Kuomintang or foreign authorities had finally succeeded in suppressing it, but because mounting disagreements between me and my Communist sponsors came to a head and the paper could not survive our break.

---

local currency by a Chinese merchant who had been alerted to expect me and I had the exhilarating experience of driving around the city of Jakarta—temporarily renamed ''Batavia'' by the Dutch in control at that time—delivering great wads of bills to the astonished and delighted wives and families of all the leading nationalist politicians who had been arrested and taken for internment, along with President Sukarno, to the small island of Banka. I had met most of them previously in Java in 1945, most memorably the oldest among them, the Muslim sage-politician Hadji Agus Salim.

* * *

I had come into this experience as a youthful neophyte, very youthful, very neophyte. But it was my good fortune to have come upon the vaccine before I encountered the virus. This happened mostly by fortuitous chance, but I must also say, even for my youthfully naive self, not entirely so. I marvel a little (with a small touch of self-congratulation) at the memory of a theme I tried to write into a play during the year of wandering on my way to China in 1930. I was working as a reporter on the *Honolulu Advertiser,* my first real post-college job, not counting the work on ships it had taken to bring me so far. There I began learning about much else in the human condition. I wrote a paper for a summer course I took at the University of Hawaii about the varieties and effects of inter-racial marriages among the Islands' many different peoples. That paper (eventually published in a festschrift presented to me by colleagues in 1976) signaled the beginning of my interest in the subject to which I eventually returned, coming to see the evolution of group identities and tribal attitudes and collisions as a prime factor in the politics of war, nationalism, and revolution to which I devoted so many of the working years of my life. But the theme I tried to turn into a play during that summer was even more directly relevant to the experience that awaited just ahead of me in China. The play was about a romantic young American radical who went to Moscow to worship at the shrine of the Revolution but found himself quite unable to accept the violence of power trampling its way toward a promised better world. In the last scene which of course I wrote first, my young hero lay abed, sick with the misery of his unwillingness to join the armed marchers outside, the great elongated shadows of their moving figures and bayonetted rifles thrown up through the windows on the slanted wall of his darkened room, the sound of their singing filling the stage. The play, if more of it had ever been written, was to be called "Tempo," meaning that it was about the pace as well as the manner in which social change had to come. Those pages did not survive, but the notions that produced them were part of the mental baggage I carried with me when I left Honolulu to go first to Manila, which I reached as a wiper in the engine room of a Dollar liner, and a few months later, as a paying passenger at last, to Shanghai before the year ended.

It was not long after my arrival there that I met Agnes Smedley. She was an intense jumpy woman, about forty then, whose public role was correspondent in China for the well-known liberal German newspaper, the *Frankfurter Zeitung,* and whose not-very-private role was that of fervent propagandist for the Communist movement in general and the Chinese Communist Party in particular. I never did know just where she was located in the Communist apparatus but I certainly did get to know that she was well in from its fringes. Besides whatever she wrote for the *Frankfurter Zeitung,* her principal outlets were in the extensive international publishing and propaganda network headed in Berlin by Willi Munzenberg, a well-known figure in the Communist movement at that time, one of whose main jobs was to mobilize "sympathizers" everywhere for the Communist, or more accurately, the Soviet cause. Agnes Smedley made a strong impression on this impressionable newcomer, but it was part of that fortuitous chance that she was a person who aroused not only interest and sympathy but also skepticism. I was ready enough, as I have indicated, to be drawn into the passions of her cause, but I also discovered that she was given to considerable exaggeration and often failed to distinguish fact from fiction, a quality I found quite characteristic of the movement into which she helped draw me. This touched other values I held high; neophyte that I was, I usually needed to take a second look.

The other larger part of that fortuitous chance came in my encounter with Frank Glass. Frank, then in his middle thirties, had served as a youthful soldier in Europe at the end of the first World War, returned to South Africa, became a Communist, was there at the time of the quickly aborted workers' uprising that took place in 1919 or 1920, the one about which, in Frank's account, Lenin, scanning the world for proletarian revolutions, is supposed to have said: "Well, South Africa has shot its bolt!" When the Communist movement split between followers of Stalin and those of Trotsky, Frank joined the latter and was expelled from the South African Communist Party in 1928. He soon left the country and wandered his way to Shanghai where we met while I was still working at the *China Press* in the spring of 1931. Frank was a tall, thin, blond man, seriously earnest about his politics and, in contrast to Agnes, measured and factual in the way he talked about it. During those riverbound talk sessions on our trip up the Yangtze, I was treated at length to his version of recent Communist history in the Soviet Union and elsewhere. His account was of course shaped by his biases, but not grossly so. It was still mostly a matter of argued differences over theory and policy. The line of blood had not yet been drawn through the Stalin-Trotsky factional struggle, not yet, at least, among the few radical foreigners who happened to come together at that far outer fringe, in Chiang Kai-shek's China, in imperialist-controlled Shanghai. It was still possible for a self-proclaimed Trotskyist like Frank Glass to consort with Stalinist types like Smedley and a German woman named Irene Weitmeyer, proprietor of the well-named Zeitgeist Bookstore, purveyor of radical European publications. Indeed, this was still long enough before the introduction of the Orwellian memory chute for the Zeitgeist Bookstore to carry not only Marxist classics but the works of both Stalin and Trotsky in several languages. Frank even worked for a time in the Shanghai bureau of Tass, the Soviet news agency. There was a spell, what's more, when he and I took turns sleeping as guards in Agnes Smedley's French Concession apartment when she thought herself threatened with a break-in by Kuomintang thugs. Frank contributed some book reviews and other writing to the *China Forum* during its short lifetime.

So it happened that through Agnes Smedley and Frank Glass and the books and pamphlets on the Zeitgeist shelves I was introduced not only to the writings of Marx and Engels but to both the Stalinist orthodox and Trotskyist oppositional Communist facts of life at the same time. What I owe to Frank Glass was the timely inoculation of better-informed skepticism and questioning reservations that I was able to bring to all that I began to learn about the history and nature of Communist politics. Frank and I remained good friends until, a few years later, at the cost of our friendship, I came to reject the Trotskyist variety of Communist politics as well as the Stalinist.

There were some heavily argued issues about China among the intra-Communist differences of which I began to become more aware at that time in Shanghai. I got my first dim view of the events that had swept and bloodied China only a few years earlier in the great sweep of the Chinese revolutionary movement of 1925-27, halted by the slaughters that accompanied Chiang Kai-shek's harsh rupture of his alliance with the Communists in April 1927, and of the role these events and differences played in the

Stalin-Trotsky split in Moscow. There were questions about the nature and strategy of the Chinese revolution, and the relative roles of the bourgeoisie, the working class, and the peasantry. I was interested and indeed would return to these matters in due course, but they had no commanding effect on me in those months after my return from upriver in the fall of 1931. I was filled with the need to *do* something about such matters as the Japanese invasion, the unsuccored dying I had seen on the Yangtze, the victims of Japan's war, and the Kuomintang's terror. The almost daily items about arrests and executions had become demands on me personally. This was what filled my mind when I eagerly took up the idea of a newspaper broached one evening at Soong Ching-ling's house and I went to work and began to produce the *China Forum*.

It was not in the columns of the *Forum* but in the under-layer of the busy two years of the *Forum's* lifetime that my differences with my Communist friends began to deepen and finally to interfere with the existence of the *Forum* itself. These differences were, again, not in the first instance about any of the issues that lay in China. I began to have more and more complicated doubts about Communist affairs elsewhere in the world, the merits of the Stalin-Trotsky struggle in Russia, and perhaps most of all, the crushing events in Germany where Stalin's insistence upon regarding the Social Democrats, not the Nazis, as the main enemy (the idea of "social fascism") had opened Hitler's road to power. (The night after Hitler took power in Berlin on January 30, 1933, a German Communist who worked for the Comintern in Shanghai, a heavy-set florid-faced man I knew only as "Harry," paced in great agitation up and down our small living room, repeating over and over again to himself: "And without a fight, without a fight!" When I saw him again a few days later, the agitation was gone. He blandly "explained" the events in Germany with the official Stalinist formula of the time which promised that Hitler's victory would be only a brief interlude on the way to Communist power in the country — "first Hitler, then us.")

I did not deal with these matters in the paper, keeping the *Forum* focused on its prime subjects, Kuomintang oppression, Japanese encroachment, Chiang's non-resistance, popular protests and strikes, the "Red armies" in the hinterland. My differences with my Communist sponsors surfaced first not in any political or ideological form but in my quite untutored resistance to untruth and exaggeration, not about the Kuomintang and its terror, which could hardly be exaggerated, but in Communist claims about their own policies and achievements. This began at the very beginning when I discovered the difference between Communist accounts abroad of the anti-Japanese resistance in the battle of Shanghai in February-March 1932, and what I had seen myself during the weeks of that now-forgotten episode. Indeed, the long report I wrote about it in the *Forum* when I could resume publishing that March was later "criticized" in a long reproachful letter-to-the-editor which I duly published.

To be sure, the paper also carried its share of unblushingly uncritical propaganda pieces about the Russian socialist fatherland and not a few overblown accounts of the "Red districts" in Kiangsi and elsewhere in central China. But it steered clear of intra-Communist politics. I simply ignored a suggestion that I publish an attack on Chen Tu-hsiu, the leader of the Party in the 1927 days, now a Trotskyist, when he was arrested and imprisoned by the Kuomintang in 1932. Instead, I was able to publish without comment a statement I extracted from the League for Civil Rights protesting his arrest. What turned out to be finally unforgivable, however, was an article I wrote in November 1933 on the sixteenth anniversary of the Russian Revolution in which I did not once mention, much less hail, our great and beloved leader Stalin. The long-developing chill in my relations with my underground sponsors turned into a freeze. At a confrontation one night that was a formal hearing, if not an actual trial, I was asked to write and publish another article that would pay proper tribute to Stalin. I said I could not. Suddenly it was all over. Fortunately for me, my judges were not in power. I went from that meeting not to a prison cell but out into that limbo of exclusion and excoriation and excommunication reserved for apostates from absolutist systems. The *Forum's* second anniversary issue had just appeared, with a note of modest self-congratulation and bold promise of more and better to come. But there was no more to come, this was the end. All support was abruptly withdrawn. There was almost no chance even to say goodbye to any of the daring young comrades who had worked for the paper at such great risk to themselves as translators and distributors. As I have indicated I never knew any of their real names, including that of the particularly devoted helper I knew as "Hsu" whom I did see when he left our apartment where he had been working and living for months. He held out his hand, tears on his cheeks, and said goodbye, adding: "I'll never believe you're a counter-revolutionary!"

A last offer of grace came from my Communist inquisitors. I could "go to the Soviet Union" and learn there how wrong I was about everything. I indignantly refused to be seduced this way, and here, surely, righteous innocence was well served. The era of the great purges was about to begin in Russia. Our virtue spared us whatever kind of moral or other liquidation might have awaited us there. Instead, we decided to liquidate our situation in Shanghai. I became not only a "counter-revolutionary" and "imperialist spy" but also a "thief" by turning over not to them but to Frank Glass the task of disposing of the small printshop I had put together and maintained with so much travail. I quit my part-time job at Havas and Viola her teaching jobs at the Ta Tsung Middle School and the University of Shanghai Night School—it was another boon of our simple-minded puritanism that we had continued to support ourselves in these jobs throughout this experience. I sent a financial SOS home and my delighted father, who had been appalled and frightened by my radical activities, came through with help that saw us through the time that followed. At the end of March 1934, we moved to Peking.

* * *

In Peking I worked for a short time as a string correspondent for the *London Daily Express* but Viola got a better job that lasted longer, teaching English in a boys' upper middle school. Our important work agenda was our own. After first completing our collection of translated short stories, of which more later, we began to fill in some of the painfully wide gaps in our knowledge of the politics in which we had been involved. We embarked in the middle of 1934 on the slow task of trying to sort out the recent history of the Communist movement in China. The eventual result was *The Tragedy of the Chinese Revolution,* a study of the revolutionary movement of 1925-27 which ended in bloody debacle and the establishment of Chiang Kai-shek's regime at Nanking, a book that was first published in London in 1938, has appeared in half a dozen languages, and is still in print, in a revised edition first published in 1951.

The work on this book began with the painstaking translation of Communist Party documents and other materials collected from various sources. It was a task that took months and was accomplished with the help of Liu Jen-ching, an early member of the Communist Party and himself a veteran of these events and of the Stalinist-Trotskyist struggles both in Russia and in China.* This made it possible for me to accumulate more than a thousand single-spaced typed pages of texts, notes, pamphlets, books, covering the events of 1925-27 and their sequels in the years that followed. It was only in this way that I began to learn for the first time of what had been going on in the Chinese Communist movement during the time of my own brief but intense apprenticeship at its fringes. It was in the course of this work, one day late in 1934, that I first learned something more about that meeting in Shanghai in 1931 where the Five Writers and those *nineteen others* were arrested. It was knowledge that came to me as a stunning discovery.

I learned that the meeting that night was an episode in a bitter factional struggle that had just come to a head inside the Communist Party leadership. Brief summary is not easy, but I must try if I am to follow the thread of this story to where it led me. When disaster struck in the spring of 1927, it came because the Chinese Communists, at Stalin's commanding behest, had subordinated themselves to the leadership of Chiang Kai-shek and the Kuomintang, a posture maintained until the very end when Chiang turned on his docile allies and cut them down, taking his terrible toll of their numbers and the people who had followed them. After a few months, again under direct orders from Moscow, the Communist Party lurched from supine accommodation to compulsive insurrection. This led during the next two years and more to one crushed uprising after another in different parts of the country, mounted by small groups isolated from a passive population. By mid-1930 it had become plain even to the Comintern that this

*Liu and his family were arrested at the Peking railroad station when they were leaving for Shanghai after his work with me was done. A friendly foreigner, Ida Pruitt, head of social work at Peking Union Medical College, was able to secure the release of his wife and children but no one else I could reach could help Liu, who disappeared into prison. I heard much later that like many other political prisoners he was freed during the Japanese war. I do not know his subsequent fate.

futile adventurism had run its course. A vacuum opened up around the issues of policy and a new leadership for the Party. This was still seen then as a leadership based on the cities of Kuomintang China, where the workers were, and not yet on the hinterland peasant armies that Chu Teh and Mao Tse-tung were gathering around them on Mao's way to taking command of the whole movement himself, a shift that did not happen until several years later. At this time in the cities there were only the shredded fragments of a workers' movement left, but the Central Committee and Politbureau of the Party were still in Shanghai heading up a gaunt skeleton-like structure of Party groups and affiliated organizations and committees.

In Shanghai on January 7, 1931, a meeting that was called the Fourth Plenum of the Central Committee was held under the eye and control of the Russian representative of the Comintern, Pavel Mif. What was left of the old leadership was brusquely deposed and Mif's protege, the Moscow-returned student Chen Shao-yu, better known later in Comintern journals as Wang Ming, was put in place as the new leader. Chen and his band of newcomers had spent the turbulent years in Moscow and had only recently returned to be given the leadership of the Party. They now shouldered aside a group of Party veterans led by Ho Meng-hsiung, a trade union leader and head of the Kiangsu Provincial Party Committee. Dismayed confusion shook the thinned ranks in Shanghai. This was the situation in which Ho Meng-hsiung and a group of his comrades, including the Five Writers, came together in that hotel on the night of January 17. Of the Five Writers only one, Li Wei-sen, twenty-eight years old, was an important Party figure with a history and a standing in the movement at a level with that of Ho Meng-hsiung, who was thirty-three. The other four Writers were junior to him in Party experience. They were all members of Shanghai groups, all followers of the leadership now so suddenly unseated by the Fourth Plenum takeover. All in the room were young, veterans not in age but of the harsh experience of the post-1927 terror and the risk and danger of trying to stay alive as Communists in the face of Kuomintang repression.

There is no hard evidence of the intentions of those who met together that night and no hard evidence of how or by whom the meeting was betrayed to the Settlement police. There are only these circumstances preceding it, the whispered rumors of deliberate betrayal that passed at the time among Party members afterward, and the cynical way in which the Communist movement went on to exploit the episode, mounting an international campaign of protest about the Five Writers and throwing a shroud of anonymity over the *nineteen others* who also died in the darkness at Lunghua. As I have already mentioned, it was not until nearly twenty years later when their bodies were exhumed and reburied that all but five of the nineteen were identified. This was long after Chen Shao-yu and his henchmen were discredited and banished back to Moscow, long after the story of the Five Writers and those who had died with them had blurred into one of the many legends of martyrdom in the Party's history, the details forgotten, only the sacrifice remembered. But it was no blurred legend for me, three years after this event that had so vividly touched my own life, when I came on those details in the obscure internal factional Party documents, mimeographed on thin paper already shredding and yellowed, uncovering to me for the first time who and what the Five and the nineteen really were and suggesting by whom and why they had been sacrificed.

Many years later this episode was closely examined by the late T.A. Hsia in his study, "The Enigma of the Five Martyrs," first published in 1962 and included in his book, *The Gate of Darkness* (Seattle, 1968). He combed every possible source and sifted the evidence with a careful and knowing hand. This evidence strongly supported, without ultimately proving, the presumptions that (1) the meeting was held to discuss how to react to the sudden replacement of the Party leadership, whether to submit or to split; and (2) that to liquidate its opposition at a single convenient stroke, the new Party leadership itself betrayed the meeting to the Shanghai police. This was the substance of my own brief treatment of the matter in *The Tragedy of the Chinese Revolution,* which T.A. Hsia cited along with much other material not then available to me. Perhaps most mordantly suggestive in his account is a passage from a review of this episode of Party history written much later by Mao Tse-tung himself in which he speaks elliptically of the "excessively severe blows" that were struck at some of the comrades involved in this affair. Hsia could ask, but found that he could not conclusively answer the question: *what* "excessively severe blows" was Mao referring to? He could hardly have meant only the displacement of individuals from Party posts or the name-calling invective that is part of all Communist factional discourse. The severest blow of all, one was left to assume, was the blow of betrayal that struck down those who died that night as the gate of darkness closed in on them at Lunghua.

As for me, I can still feel now what I felt that afternoon in 1934 in that quiet room of our house in Peking, the documents spread on my desk, Liu reading them in English translation for me to type, suddenly rammed hard by the severe blow of truths I had not known were there when I moved among them. It was the discovery of a depth of cynicism I had not dreamed was possible, grossly magnified by the indication of deliberate betrayal but gross enough even without this in the way the fate of the Five had been made the cause of compassionate protest while the nineteen were left nameless and the rest of the story remained untold by them and, in all my innocence, by me when I wrote of their martyrdom in the pages of the *China Forum*. Unlike the victims at Lunghua, I did not have to pay for such innocence with my life, only with a piece of my youth and of the naivete I had shared with them and which they paid so heavily to keep intact to the end.

Out of all this came, then, the crowded jumble of feelings and memories rolling back across all the screens and registers of my mind as Viola and I stood nearly fifty years later on that wet and chilly afternoon before the grave of these Five and the nineteen at the Cemetery of the Martyrs in Shanghai. Here were the well-remembered Five Writers, Jou Shih, twenty-nine, Li Wei-sen, twenty-eight, Huh Yeh-pin, twenty-seven, Feng Kung, a woman, twenty-four, and Yin Fu, twenty-two. Of the "nineteen others," left nameless for so many years, here were seven, with pictures and names, led by Ho Meng-hsiung, a veteran at thirty-three, and the six others, all identified as Party workers in various Shanghai committees: Lin Yu-nan, also thirty-three, Lung Ta-tao, thirty, Wu Chung-wen, a woman, twenty-eight, Wang Ching-shih, twenty-four, Li Wen, a woman, twenty-one, and Ou-Yang Li-An, twenty, who, the brief biographical note said, had come to Shanghai in 1928, a survivor of the slaughters in Changsha, in Hunan, where his career as a revolutionist had begun in 1925 when he was fourteen. And here, without pictures but named at last, were seven more, ages not given but all presumably of that same generation of young Party members, all also identified as workers in various Shanghai groups: Yun Yu-tang, Tsai Po-chen, Ah Kang, Fei Ta-fu, Peng Yen-keng, Tang Shih-lun, and Tang Shih-chuan. Only the last five of the twenty-four bodies exhumed from the ground at the Garrison Headquarters remained nameless in this history, like the many thousands of others who died in Shanghai in 1927 and afterward at the hands of Chiang Kai-shek's Kuomintang executioners.

We stood there silent for some minutes, the rain dripping down around us from the edges of our umbrellas. Then we walked back to the low plain building that housed a small exhibit. It included blown-up pictures of the victims and, under glass, the remnants of a blue sweater that had been worn by Feng Kung on that last night and which had somehow survived the years in the ground. A photo of her wearing that sweater, which had served as a key to the identification of the remains, was also on display. A piece of Russian-style sculpture depicted the Five going to their death. I felt some small sense of loss appeased to see the pictures and the names, victims not only retrieved from a hidden grave but brought back from the bottom of a Communist memory chute.

Back in the director's office to sip tea before leaving, I questioned our hosts, officials of the cemetery, and found, as I expected, that they knew little or nothing of the history buried under that plain stone. They were able to tell me of the special effort that had been made to locate and dig up the bodies of these twenty-four people, but they knew nothing about any other remains of all the other victims executed at the same place. They said that the men who fled the Kuomintang Garrison Headquarters when the Communist army approached the city in 1949 had burned or otherwise disposed of their records. As far as I could learn, nothing had ever been done about any other victims. Was there any monument anywhere, I asked, to the thousands who had died on the streets of Shanghai in 1927 or those killed by Chiang's executioners in the years that followed? No one in the room had an answer. They looked blank, puzzled, or just possibly—my own projection, no doubt—embarrassed. These Communist functionaries, some of them forty and fifty years old, either did not know what I was talking about or did not see why such a monument should exist. The director referred to a monument in Peking which he said was for *all* the martyrs of the Revolution, and that would obviously include those I seemed to have in mind. They gave me a booklet about the martyrs buried in this place. It included pictures of half a dozen or so individuals dating from 1925 and 1927, remembered in this booklet but apparently not buried here. Outside in the open courtyard in front of the building, some young men who seemed to be part of the cemetery's staff were listlessly playing basketball in the drizzle, a few others looking on. They turned their heads to watch us leave and went back to their game. It did not appear to be a place overrun by visiting crowds, only by an over-large staff with nothing to do.

I asked to be driven to the site of the Shanghai-Woosung Garrison Headquarters, not far away, along a crowded winding road that went past the Lunghua Pagoda, one of Shanghai's prime tourist sights. We stopped outside a black gate in a long gray wall. This was the place. I had never seen it, never dared to go out to it in those days. Now it was a small-arms repair shop operated by the army, I was told. I was invited to inspect it, but no, I said, I did not need to go inside, only to sit a moment and look at that huge black gate, the original gate of the place, they said. It could have been a representation of Lu Hsun's "gate of darkness," the gate of the Tang legend which he used to say it was his task to hold open so that the young could pass through it into the light. I felt again what I had felt one day a few years before, standing in front of the Lubianka, the dread headquarters of the secret police in Moscow. All the dead, I thought, all the dead. All *that,* I thought, looking around me, for *this?* It was to look for a moment into history's maw. How many were there anywhere, I wondered as we drove back into the city, to share the memory of fear and terror and loss and defiance that gripped so many people who had passed this way in those years now so soon forgotten? And where will anyone go to bow one's head for all the victims added to them in all the years since the Communists freed the country from the Kuomintang regime and replaced it with their own?

*   *   *

It remains here to tell how we happened to make this journey of re-encounter. This too must take us back to more of these beginnings and some of what followed.

The translated short stories by Chinese writers that appeared in the *China Forum* in 1932 and 1933 attracted the attention of a well-known New York publisher who wrote expressing interest in a book-length collection. I sought the counsel of Lu Hsun and he and Mao Tun, then already one of the best known of the younger writers, began the process of choosing the stories to be included. When the *Forum* was cut off, this was still unfinished business. Lu Hsun, who had difficulties of his own dealing with our mutual friends the Communists, was not one to be put off by the fact that they were now applying to me some of the choice epithets in the Communist polemical vocabulary. Overnight I had become a "counter-revolutionary Trotskyist," an "imperialist agent," an "American and/or Japanese spy." Lu Hsun, for his part, gave us a farewell dinner before we left Shanghai, as we were reminded by an entry in his diary called to our attention during our recent return. When we left Shanghai that March of 1934, we carried with us a folder full of stories to be translated and there were still choices to be made of others to be included. Through that spring, letters passed between us dealing with the problems of selection and the work of translation, which we were completing with a Chinese translator, a "Miss Yang," as we knew her, who, if I remember correctly, had been sent to us by Lu Hsun for this task. By summer, the work was done and the manuscript, called *Straw Sandals,* from a line in a Lu Hsun essay, was shipped off to New York.

But we soon learned that the New York publisher's enthusiasm, unlike Lu Hsun's, had evaporated on discovering that I was now carried on the Communist index as an enemy of the people. It was a dollars-and-cents problem for him. It meant he could not count on the "special support"—usually the assured cost-covering sale of 1,000 or more copies—which the Communists in New York used so successfully in those days to influence publishers. Whether because this "special support" was lacking in my case—as one publishing house unashamedly informed me in its letter of rejection—or because these stories were not then seen as commanding publishable interest on their own, the book was turned down by publisher after publisher during the next two years. It was finally left to rest in our files along with the folder of our correspondence with Lu Hsun and Mao Tun. I have told elsewhere the story of that book and its writers and its eventual publication.* What is to the point here is that those letters written to me in 1934 by Lu Hsun

*See my Introduction to *Straw Sandals: Chinese Stories 1918-1933,* M.I.T. Press, Cambridge, Mass., 1974.

and Mao Tun led, through a succession of chances, to the invitation that took us back to China in 1980.

In the nearly forty years they lay away all but forgotten, wars and revolutions transformed the world's power systems, including China's. My own experience of this time included a return to China as a correspondent during the Second World War. It turned out to be for me also a resumption of my own hostilities with Chiang Kai-shek's government, or at least with its censors. I and some other correspondents would in some cases evade Chinese censorship by flying across the Hump to India to file our stories from there. One such occasion was the time in late 1944 that General Joseph Stilwell was recalled from his China command at Chiang Kai-shek's request, a story in which I referred to Chiang's regime as "a government in exile in its own country." This was one of the particulars laid against me a few months later when on returning from a brief home leave, I was barred by the Chungking government from re-entering China. That was in mid-1945 and had the effect of deflecting me after Japan's surrender to the Philippines, Japan, Korea, and then to the beginnings of the nationalist wars in Indochina and Indonesia, all of this duly reported to *Newsweek* and in a 1947 book called *No Peace for Asia.*

In the years that followed there were more journeys, more writing, more books, a change of venue from journalism to academia, and a shift in focus from politics as such to the perceptions of groups of people caught up in its changes. This became a series of studies based on extensive interviewing of people of many kinds in different places whose identities and sense of themselves had been wrenched around and transformed in so many ways by the political and social convulsions of these years. One book was about American perceptions of China and India. Others were about black and white Americans in Africa, black Americans in America, Jewish Americans in Israel, ex-untouchables in India. There were additional inquiries concerning .English-educated Chinese in Malaysia, young people in the Philippines and Japan. All of this was eventually brought together in 1975 in a book called *Idols of the Tribe* which was about the nature of group identity itself and its persistent role in history and in all our contemporary affairs at home and in the world.

For twenty-three of these years, after 1949, China was closed off from contact with America and Americans, but even after the re-opening in 1972, it remained closed to me. The arch anti-imperialist Mao Tse-tung and the arch anti-Communist Richard Nixon could shake hands. But there was no statute of limitations on my crimes, at least not then, in the heyday of the so-called Cultural Revolution, as Soong Ching-ling, now holding exalted office in the Communist regime, discovered when she tried to invite us to "see the new China." Someone in Peking, with more authority than she had ever had, told her brusquely that I was a "traitor" and "should never be invited." That was in 1974, the year *Straw Sandals* was published. Its stories had acquired considerable historic as well as literary interest and, I belatedly realized, so had the letters from Lu Hsun and Mao Tun, all the more because they were handwritten. This was true of the Lu Hsun letters particularly, since everything his hand ever touched was being collected in China as part of the national treasure. Lu Hsun was long dead (he died in 1936) and his differences with the Communists over the role of writers and writing in politics had long been buried with him. The much less prickly and more amenable Mao Tun had become Minister of Culture in the Communist government, but he too disappeared, in 1965, into the limbo created by Mao's Gang of Four during the Cultural Revolution; when I tried to send him a copy of *Straw Sandals,* it came back stamped "Addressee Unknown." But these letters, in any case, obviously belonged in some more permanent place than our filing cabinet and I presented them that year to the Harvard-Yenching Library in Cambridge.

Eugene Wu, the Harvard-Yenching librarian, subsequently sent copies of these letters to the institutes in Peking and Shanghai where Lu Hsun material was being collected and studied. It was from that turbulent sea upon which they had been cast that they came back to me on a summer afternoon in 1980 when two Chinese friends brought me a copy of a Chinese literary journal, the *Hsin Hua Yueh Pao,* in which they were published, along with other recent findings from Lu Hsun's pen. Their appearance in this form came to me as surprise enough—I did not know until then that copies had been sent to China—but much more remarkable, I quickly discovered, were the explanatory notes someone had written to accompany them. These had two extraordinary features: they were impeccably accurate and, most extraordinary of all, my name appeared in them with no derogatory labels attached. This was a change at the low bottom of things that clearly reflected a change at the high top.

Mao Tse-tung died in 1976 and soon thereafter his wife Chiang Ching and her principal cohorts, now known as the "Gang of Four," were outmaneuvered in their reach for the succession, were arrested, and charged with great crimes against the Revolution. This ushered in a process of change whose nature and scope were still unclear. Most American observers of China (as I had undertaken to show in a 1958 book called *Scratches on Our Minds)* usually went to extremes in their biases about China and the Chinese. The majority tended to belong in more recent times to the lo-the-wonder-of-it school, and none more so than most of those who wrote about the Communist regime, including many who told us during the nightmarish assaults of the Cultural Revolution that Mao and his "Thoughts" and his wife and her friends were performing all kinds of miracles of transformation, including the creation of a new species of man. Mao's death and the downfall of his wife and her friends certainly did usher in a period of change in Chinese affairs and it was obviously going to take time to see what would now emerge from all the unsettled dust. However, here before me now was evidence that some of this change, whatever its larger scope or possible duration, could reach all the way to me. It was enough to move me to write a letter to the editor of that journal to say that we were going to be in Japan in October and that if there was any interest in our doing so, Viola and I would be glad to come on to Peking for a brief visit. I wrote to Soong Ching-ling to the same effect.

Only a few days before we were due to take plane to Tokyo, our phone rang at a late evening hour. It was a wire from the Writers Association in Peking cordially inviting us to come to China as their guests, adding that if we wired our acceptance, they would have visas waiting for us at the Chinese embassy in Tokyo. We wired our acceptance.

Tokyo, October 11

I went to the Chinese Communist embassy today in a Japanese Foreign Office car to pick up our visas before our departure to Peking day after tomorrow. This came about simply because a friend who is a high official in the Foreign Office took us to lunch.

When we left the Ginza restaurant, his long black official car was waiting at the curb and he asked where we were bound. Viola said she was staying downtown to do some errands and she took off down the street. I said I had to go to the Chinese embassy, whereupon our friend waved me into the car and we drove first to the Foreign Office where he got out, instructing the driver to take me on to the embassy and then back to the International House where we were staying. So it was that I was driven on alone, head back against the cushion, marvelling at this comic circumstance, wondering how I could ever convey just how comic, how bizarre it was, how it showed again that the more some things change they are and are not quite the same, how big somber feelings can dissolve into small funny things, how every image on this journey must blur into a double exposure.

For it so happens that we traveled from Japan to Peking once before, in 1933, when the political topography was so utterly different, the quake-like scope of changes to come quite beyond imagining, when the presence of a Chinese Communist embassy in Tokyo was all but inconceivable, and the only official car that would and did take us anywhere belonged to the Japanese political police, guardians of the land against all bringers of what were called "dangerous thoughts." Japan was ruled by its militarists, already embarked on their course of conquest, beginning in China. China was ruled by Chiang Kai-shek and assorted regional generals. The Chinese Communists were small bands of fugitive guerrillas in Central China mountain hideouts or scattered squads of beleaguered Party militants underground in a few cities. Powerful or weak, all makers of politics feed on dreams. Japan's generals and admirals were dreaming of becoming masters of all Asia and the world, and we, two obscure young new recruits to the dream-world of the Revolution, had our contrary vision of how human affairs might be ordered. Since this took the form in our small paper in Shanghai of advocating resistance to the Japanese invaders and denouncing Chiang Kai-shek's non-resistance, we were met, when our steamer docked at Nagasaki, by a delegation of Japanese political policemen who wanted to know why we had come to Japan.

We told them the truth, which was that we had come from Shanghai to spend a vacation—actually it was a delayed honeymoon trip—to try to glimpse what Japan was like. We had in fact come out of a certain perverse curiosity. Having seen Japanese only in China, mostly as invading soldiers, sailors, armed civilians, I wanted to see what Japanese were like in Japan. This was obviously an unbelievable lie. A police interrogation was needed to get at some more plausible truth. At the beginning, I rather enjoyed the exchange. Having tested my radical-diplomatic style in encounters with American officials in Shanghai, I fancied myself a match for Japanese police agents whose humorless heavyhandedness was the stuff of funny stories at every foreign bar in China. I saw myself as suave and cool and clever, turning aside all political questions, insisting I had left all such matters behind me in Shanghai, inviting them to come to visit me there to discuss anything they wished. We had come, I told them, because Japan was said to be a beautiful land and we wanted to see it for ourselves. But as the hours passed in the empty steamer saloon, the repetitive duel ceased to be amusing, especially after they went through our baggage with numbing thoroughness, shaking out every folded piece of clothing, even squeezing out tubes of toothpaste. We had just about concluded that they were not going to let us land when our principal inquisitor told us we could go, but that we could travel only on the island of Kyushu and on the Inland Sea, not to any principal cities. When we finally descended the gangway with our manhandled belongings, I did so angrily muttering that we would never come back to Japan until after the Revolution.

In what followed, however, aggravation soon dissolved back into comedy. They thought us important enough to dog our every step but in less than a day's time, for their own greater convenience I am sure, they took not to following us but leading us wherever they were ready to let us go. The mostly hilarious result was a police-conducted tour during which we were politely handed over from one escort to another who not only made sure that we did, saw, and heard nothing subversive, but also carried our bags, made our train and boat bookings, bought our tickets, solicitously advised us as to the best inns and restaurants, guided us to the choicest viewing spots at the best sights, or pursued us, as one of them had to do, panting and sweating, fanning himself fiercely with his straw hat, as we scampered up the long stone step path to the top of the mountain in the center of the holy island of Miyajima. From the top of that mountain we looked across the narrow stretch of gleaming sea at the small city where we had taken the ferry to come to this famous place. We did not note or remember that city's name at the time. It was not until thirty years later when we came again to Miyajima on a sentimental journey that we realized that the city whose name we did not know was Hiroshima.

Miyajima was as far as we got into Japan that first time so long ago. With its great red torii, or gate, standing with its feet in the green water, it was like a travel poster scene of beauty and tranquillity without possible connection to the ugly and violent Japanese scene in China. We quickly discovered that Miyajima itself mirrored the contrast. Only half of the island was holy, given over to its ancient temple, its chanting priests and pious pilgrims. The other half was a military reservation where no one could go. Indeed, we gave our police guide a hard time that day by taking the wrong way down the mountain, losing both him and ourselves in the process. We saw nothing military, only one aged fisherman who looked like a figure in a Hiroshige print, who needed hardly any of our sign language to understand our plight and who drew a map in the sand to show us how to get back to our inn at the edge of the water on the island's holy, or safe side.

Duly back in tow, we were delivered some days later by train to Shimonoseki, where the treaty ending the first Sino-Japanese war in 1895 ceded Formosa (Taiwan) to Japan, and then by steamer across the Japan Sea to Dairen, the south Manchurian port seized from the Russians as spoils of victory in the Russo-Japanese War of 1905. In Dairen we saw an exposition which featured a large wall covered by a huge Japanese rising sun flag, rows of electric bulbs along its great spreading rays, coming alight in stages, first over Manchuria, then over China Proper, then over most of Asia westward and eastward over the Pacific and finally, all lights ablaze by this time, over the United States as far east as the Mississippi or thereabouts—they did not seem to plan to take Chicago. This was the vision of the future we carried with us aboard the steamer that took us to Tientsin where we took the train to Peking. We had also been able to see, however, that not all Japanese, not even all Japanese political policemen, were necessarily rampaging monsters, and that some things funny could somehow lie wrapped in something so baleful, so full of hate, violence, and fear.

I did come back to Japan after revolutionary changes had taken place, though not the kind I had in mind that day on the gangway in Nagasaki. It was in 1945 only days after the surrender when the country lay shattered in defeat, and Hiroshima and Nagasaki lay leveled in the worst the future had brought. We came again much later when Japan had begun to rise from its ashes to reach toward world economic primacy, a goal it paradoxically took a great defeat, not a conquering victory, to achieve. The emperor was still in his palace and the tycoons were busy in their great new company complexes, but the politics of the country were no less democratic than the most democratic anywhere, and Japanese mastery was plain in many brand new ways, well past Chicago, past Detroit, and in parts of the globe those Dairen dreamers never dreamed of in their military-bound universe. In the years that China was closed to Americans, we came back to Japan a number of times, on journeys of inquiry, for lectures and seminars, as indeed we had this time when we came to take part in a conference and to have reunions with a considerable circle of friends. I remember after we left Japan on one of those visits looking across into Communist China from the last closed barrier on Hong Kong territory, musing over the shifts of role and place in our scheme of things: the Japan we once knew as the closed enemy land now part of the open world where we passed freely among friends, the China with which we had identified ourselves now closed behind walls of separation. Now, in another one of those large turnings in politics, it had opened again, even for us. In a day's time, we fly from here to Peking, coming again from Japan, but such a different Japan, to such a different China, and we two, made by the years into two such different people.

Tokyo to Peking, October 13

It is a sensation unlike any I have ever had on any journey before. We have headed often into unknowns of one kind or another. The feeling was always one of expectancy and exhilaration, of pending discovery, of who and what waited to be met, seen, heard, learned, experienced, new questions to be asked, new answers to be grasped. This is all here now still but in a different setting of emotions shaken loose, memories swarming up around them, of coming around in a circle to revisit my own past. All this and more churns in me at this moment on our way back to Peking, back to China.

We had occasion a few years ago to visit Moscow for the first time. That too, like this one, was a journey attended by the shades of emotions past, all the associations my generation has had with the revolutionary vision that rose and fell there. It was a place to mourn in, and so we did, standing silently across from the Lubianka where so many died at the hands of Stalin's G.P.U. Behind us in a big department store for children's things, voracious shoppers grabbed at the sparse and shoddy goods available there, symbols of the outcome for which all this dying had been done. But the meaning of what had happened in Russia had come to us across a distance. In China we had touched something of this experience ourselves and come to know a little of the risk and pain that went with it for those engaged in its commitments and its harshness. It was in China that I was initiated into adulthood, a kind of political puberty rite ending in the loss of my political youth if not yet quite all my illusions. It was in China also, even more crucially, that we two began our lives together, another initiation into a maturity of a more enduring kind. The political theme in this fugue of ours played itself out through the years into a haunted vacancy of confusion and unsolved riddles. But the other, our own, rising out of our two selves, grew and deepened, playing ever more strongly against the bleakness of the human condition around us. Such is the uniqueness in our own lives of the place to which this huge plane is carrying us. It is the piace where, for us, all this began.

* * *

Coming from Tokyo's jammed Narita airport to Peking's new, large, but empty airport was a little like coming to another planet. There were only four other planes on the ground when we landed. Our planeload of passengers, mostly eager Japanese businessmen, made a small lonely file as we moved through the vacant vastness of the terminal. We were met by a soft-spoken smiling man of about sixty, Li Shin of the Writers Association who introduced himself to us as our host for the visit, and Ho Pin, a tall young woman of thirty who was to serve as interpreter. They greeted us cordially, put our bags in the trunk of their car, and we drove off down the broad treelined road to the city we last saw forty-five years ago. On the road with us were a few other cars, some trucks, many bicycles, and, most of all, people on foot. On the way in, Li Shin told us there would be a Writers Association dinner in our honor that evening, hosted by Ting Ling. Tomorrow evening we were invited to dinner by Soong Ching-ling.

They took us to the Beijing Hotel, the old Grand Hotel de Pekin, now flanked on both sides by buildings added in more recent years, filled now, even as it used to be when we lived in Peking, by foreigners only. In our time here, we rarely came to this elegant hostelry. I remember once we stopped in for a cool drink and were shocked at having to pay the equivalent of fifty cents for an orange juice. Now, solicitously guided through the jam of visitors and tourists, we were taken up to a spacious room on the twelfth floor and left there to rest a bit before dinner. Outside our window, looking west to the hills to which we used to ride on our bicycles, the city stretched away over the tops of a succession of the ugly squat square buildings put up in such numbers during the regime's Russian period, and no wall. The ancient wall that used to rim the old city was gone. The grayness ran unbroken to the far outskirts where clusters of smokestacks, one after another, belched their black stuff into the sky, covering the blue we knew must be there but could not see behind the thick smog.

*　*　*

Dinner was at a duck restaurant on a downtown street. The picture of a duck restaurant in our minds—double exposure again—was the Lao Bien-i-fong, centuries old, it was said, where we used to go with friends, choose our duck on entering the courtyard, then mount to one of the many private dining rooms on upper floors and, drinking tea, wait for it to come to us in all its parts and savory splendor. But here now, in a plainer place, waiting to greet us was Ting Ling, a short, broad, gray woman, seventy-seven years old, with clipped hair, a round lined face, and tired eyes, who gave us each a great hug. And here, a surprise of which we had learned on the ride in from the airport, was one of our oldest China friends, Chen Han-seng, aged and frail, nearly blinded by cataracts in both eyes, another big embrace, words of welcome, and a waiting party of other guests, strangers to us. They all turned out to be connected in one way or another to Lu Hsun: his daughter-in-law, Ma Shin-yun, who explained to us that her husband, Lu Hsun's son, was out of town and would come to call in a few days; Li Hu-lin, director of the Lu Hsun Museum in Peking; a younger man, Ko Pao-chuan, introduced as a leading Lu Hsun scholar; and others, professors, writers, members of institutes of literature, language, and the social sciences. One of them, a round-faced man named Tang Tao, smilingly volunteered: "We were neighbors in Shanghai." He worked, he said, at the post office, a long block or so down from the apartment house on Soochow Creek where we lived. "I used to read the *China Forum* there," he said. "That was when I began to write."

There were toasts of welcome, much said about old friends coming together again. Most of the talk that followed was about Lu Hsun and my connection with him. It was this connection, it began to seem, for which all this honor was being shown me. I tried to ask some questions, of Ting Ling what she was writing now, or Han-seng about himself, but quickly had to give up in the convivial confusion, making appointments instead to see them in coming days. We had not known what to expect of this welcome, we had not expected it to be so friendly or so opaque. But the oddity was wrapped in warmth we let roll over us, the welcoming enthusiasm, the air of celebration, even though we were not sure what was being celebrated or what friendship was being hailed by these reunited good friends.

I must gracelessly add that while the food was good enough, though not as good as we remembered such food to be, we were dismayed by what went with it to drink. One always drank tea at Chinese tables, and warmed white wine in tiny cups, the best of it from Shaoshing in Chekiang south of Shanghai. Here we were offered the brutally hard grain drink, mao-tai, beer, a sweet red wine, Coke, a positively execrable bottled sweet orange drink, and no tea, which we had to ask for and which arrived in Western style teacups. (We found this assortment the rule at all tables, public or private, at which we sat during our visit; in both symbolic and painfully real terms, it was one of the more distressing examples of "modernization.")

The evening ended early. Puzzled and bemused, yet pleased, we were ushered back to our hotel. It had been much like a welcome to a returning prodigal, his old sins left unmentioned.

Peking, October 14

This was a day of retracing old steps, of not coming home again.

The year and a half we lived in Peking in 1934-35 was like a small hole in time. Chiang Kai-shek had managed to drive his Communist foes to the far northwest, but his regime was weak and faltering. It was suffering from its own inner rot, the blows of the world economic depression, and the Japanese invasion of the northeastern provinces. Japanese forces stood at the Jehol border, only a few hundred miles from Peking. Large events were at a pause. Japan's advance into north China itself did not begin until mid-1937. In this interval when so relatively little happened and so much was pending, we lived a small idyll of our own in this place. We could do so because Peking was a city of such age and beauty in all its seasons, because we were privileged foreigners who could remain in fact if not in feeling exempt from the blows of the more common fortune, because we were deep in work, my writing and Viola's teaching, that we valued and thought important, most of all because we were so young and so much in love. This made us marvelously self-sufficient, and a good thing it was, because there was no community, no group, no circle of which we could easily become part.

Peking in the 1930s was a place where the past set the tone and pace for much of the daily life of its people. This was also largely true in different ways of the foreigners who lived there. The diplomatic and consular establishment was for the most part itself a relic of the past, like the old Legation Quarter in which it existed, living on ground that was eroding under it. Most of the non-official foreigners in the city, unlike the commercially absorbed foreign community in Shanghai, were in Peking pursuing religious, cultural, academic interests. But these interests were mainly focused on times and matters distant from the current Chinese reality. Our intense and radical interest in the here-and-now made us something of an oddity among them. Some of our best friends, however, were academics, like John and Wilma Fairbank, and there were others, among the correspondents and even a few junior diplomats, with whom we could share time and talk. At the same time, we were cut off from whatever of our kind of politics existed in Peking. It was all there, including the political police, prisons, and a small underground trying to fan the embers of the anti-Japanese movement; but we were unwelcome mavericks or dangerous friends best to avoid in those quarters, or for that matter, in more respectable Chinese quarters as well. Still, we made the best of it in the space and time we had, we worked hard, played joyously, and gave ourselves up to the magic that was then still part of the experience of living in Peking.

The city in which this was possible is gone and not to be found anywhere here now, not in its great surviving monuments of long-past Chinese glory, not in its massively ugly new buildings, not in its smothering new industry, in the new shapes of its ruling power, or in the vision of greater well-being held out before its much larger numbers of people. Walking in a Chinese city was never an uncrowded experience, but in this capital city now where automobile traffic is still sparse and thin on its great avenues, it was like plunging into a thick and restlessly moving human stream. On shop-lined Wangfuching Ta Chieh, we were able to stay in it only for a few blocks. In the park around Pei Hai, the lake in the Forbidden City, we walked among thousands of fellow strollers, adults in their somber blues, blacks, grays, the young a bit less severely covered, and the children, in long lines following teachers or little ones with parents or grandparents, in high color, reds and yellows and greens and whites, all here seeking respite, the pleasure of openness, of trees, grass, flowers. From living quarters where families were jammed into one or two tiny rooms in this grimly overcrowded city, a walk in the park, even following each other in such numbers on each others' heels, seemed to be the nearest people could get to being by themselves. (Our young interpreter Ho Bin, herself part of a rather well-situated Party middle-establishment family, one day described the smallness of the space in which she and her husband and child lived with her husband's mother, her sister-in-law and her husband and child. We asked her what she did for privacy. She did not know the English word. When we explained what it meant, she smiled brightly and said: "Oh, when I want privacy I go for a walk in the park!") Once in the middle of the heavy sauntering traffic on one path, I saw a young father crouched next to his small daughter in light green and white, pointing up to the top of the White Pagoda rising high above us, his square ugly beautiful face creased with the effort to explain to her what it was, she looking up at it and then at him with utter intentness, trying to understand what he was saying. We stood still at the edge of the stream of passersby taking it in, until he looked up and saw us watching him and with an embarrassed smile scooped up his little girl and disappeared with her into the moving crowd.

Pei Hai is where we used to go ice skating in winter. We looked vainly for the place where we would clump up on our skates on a board platform to a small enclosed foodstall where we ate steaming *roh-mor,* hot spiced minced meat, served in a warm *shao-ping,* or roll, drank hot tea, warming our hands around our cups, before clumping back out onto the ice to skate some more under the late afternoon sky. (We learned on inquiry that *roh-mor* and *shao-ping* could be ordered as part of a meal at an elaborate restaurant in a pavilion at the lake's edge, open to foreign visitors only. We went back a few days later and had some. Obviously, it was not the same.) Walking at seventy among our masses of fellow strollers, we were seeing ourselves at twenty-three, so young in this old place, full of the joy of exertion, of breathing the frigid air, of holding hands and skating together in the face of the cold, finally regaining our bikes and wheeling back to our house in the *hutung* a few miles away.

This time we rejoined our car and waiting hosts at the outer gate and went looking for the school at which Viola taught that year, the first foreigner and the first woman ever to teach there. It was the Hopeh Provincial Upper Middle School for Boys, housed in what had once been part of some Manchu court establishment at the northern edge of the Forbidden City beyond Coal Hill. Its classes met in low Peking red buildings with curved tile roofs, surrounding several large stone-paved courtyards alight in spring and summer with flowers planted in plots among the stones. On ordinary days, the school was a fifteen-minute bicycle ride from our house in the East City. But on the days when the wind blew in hard from the Gobi, it would take her more than a half hour of hard pedaling to cover the distance each morning. Afternoons, however, she would come almost literally sailing home before the wind, back at our large red door in less than ten minutes. In winter she went bundled in her Chinese padded gown and trousers and fleece-lined shoes, knitted helmet, its visor across her face. Students at first would line up to look at this young foreign woman in her old-fashioned plebeian Chinese garb, but they soon got used to her, as they did to the closing off of one section of the all-boys' school latrine-style toilet reserved for her during her hours there.

There was no school of its old-style name any more and we had to go looking for anyone who might remember it. The search took us through neighborhoods not on any sightseeing routes, shabby crowded streets filled with busy people working, as people here always had, at a thousand hard-done tasks, where there was little or no new construction or "modernization" to be seen. It took

Viola with her class at middle school, Peking, 1934

many stops and inquiries, but we finally found what we were look-ing for, a surviving remnant of the old school building, its remain-ing tiles faded, paint peeling, close to a "new" normal school. The school principal, who received us with instant grace and courtesy, told us this "new" building had been built in 1954. It was badly run down, its cemented brick walls stained and crumbling, looking even more decrepit than the remnant of the old school still stand-ing next to it. It was not the kind of school put on circuit for foreign visitors. There was no one around who had been part of the Hopeh Provincial Upper Middle School for Boys, he told us, but the school was remembered, he said, because so many of its students became heroic fighters in the War of Liberation. Viola well remembered the strained silence that greeted her queries one day about the absence of one of the boys in her class that year. After class, several boys came up to her and whispered that he had been taken away by the police because he was suspected of being a "Communist." The little we had begun to hear about the present generation of young people in Peking made us wonder what filled the heads of boys that age in such a school here now.

*   *   *

This afternoon we went back to the house we lived in at No. 1 Ta Yang Yi Ping Hutung in the East City. By another of the many chances attending this journey, we walked there with Wilma Fairbank who also happened to be visiting in Peking this week. We first met Wilma and John Fairbank in Shanghai in 1932 when they too were newly wed, and again in Peking when we visited the city the next year. It was Wilma, when we came here to live early in 1934, who helped us to find this house, just a short way down from theirs on this narrow street that ended not far from the city wall that marked the eastern boundary of the old imperial capital. Wilma, student of the arts and artist herself, and John, graduate student of history on his way to becoming a leading figure in Chinese studies in America, were the best of neighbors and friends we had during that brief Peking interlude in our young lives.

The house we lived in lay out of sight behind the gray walls that lined both sides of the unpaved hutung, low structures with gray tiled roofs set around courtyards surrounded by walls, passages between them made and unmade down the many years for smaller or larger dwelling places for people whose affluence or importance could be measured by how many rooms, or *chien,* and courtyards they occupied. A *chien* was a space about ten feet square. The typical house section facing a courtyard might be made up of three or more *chien.* The house we rented had the equivalent of about 14 *chien* in all, I think, in three main quadrangular sections separated by courtyards or passages. The front nearest the street for kitchen and servant quarters (first occupied by our cook and friend, Ching, a Kiangsu man who came with us from Shanghai but left in a few months having been forced to conclude that "these Hopeh people don't speak like Chinese, don't behave like Chinese, don't eat Chinese food, they're not Chinese at all!"). The second formed our dining and living room. Then came the main court-

Dancing in our courtyard, Peking, 1934

yard, measuring perhaps 25 by 35 feet, where we took our meals in good weather at a red table with red benches under a lovely bending tree next to flower beds laid among the stones. Here Viola practiced her Chinese dancing, swinging swords or spear, or gliding through the fluid movements of *wu-shu,* one form of Chinese shadow boxing, taking lessons from her teacher, Mr. Li, a man of incomparable athletic grace whose family had been dancers for many generations. Facing the far side of this courtyard was the section of our living quarters, divided into a study, a tiny bedroom, and a bath newly installed for our benefit, its equipment all made out of that speckled gray cement used in basement sinks of not-so-new houses at home, including a marvel of a long narrow bathtub in which we used to gambol and over which we created a shower, a sensational fixture on this street, out of pipes and the head of a sprinkling can. Back of this section ran a narrow passage ending at a last small room that stood by itself against the back wall. All in all, the inside living space in our house was equivalent to six modest-sized rooms and the courtyard space equalled the lawn and yard around a house that size on a plot 25 by 100 feet, no mansion, clearly, but a dream of a house in which to live an idyll.

And so we did. Viola biked out to school mornings. Afternoons one or both of us pedaled to the libraries we scoured for materials in books or newspaper files, at the once-great Peking National University or in the smaller but helpfully filled stacks of the Peking Language School. I worked long hours at my desk, first with a translator on the stories that went into *Straw Sandals* and then with Liu Jen-ching on our file of Communist and other Chinese materials. Late in the day we would often go walking atop the nearby city wall, high enough to see what could not be seen from the street, green treetops rising above all the gray roofs. We walked there on soft evenings when the sky was filled with color, and sometimes at night when the entire firmament around us was shattered by distant lightning breaking in great sheets out of the darkness. On occasion we would bike out to marketplaces, or to a movie, or to the YMCA to dissipate with a wicked chocolate sundae. We took a longer trip once with the Fairbanks, jouncing in the back of an old Dodge truck up to the Great Wall, through the pass at Kupeikow and, after some delay at a Japanese checkpoint, on into occupied Jehol and to its capital, Chengteh, returning by river and rail to Peking.

The river trip took us for five days down the swiftly running current through the gorges of the Luan River in a small boat expertly navigated by our boatman, Mr. Hao, and his crew of two small boys. Mr. Hao, a man of grace and master of his environment, stopped at his village, a tiny cluster of small houses perched on the riverbank, to show us where he lived and, mainly, to exhibit his unusual passengers to his family and fellow villagers. He was puzzled, amused, and dismayed by what he learned about the culture and habits of these creatures from another world, such as the fact we were each one husband to one wife only and that the same was true of everyone. "Even the officials?" he asked in disbelief. Mr. Hao could not see why, when we tied up at the bank each evening, we refused the comfort of the bottom of his boat under its woven bamboo canopy and took our blankets up on shore instead to sleep there. Why so, asked Mr. Hao. "We like to see the stars," one of us replied, "don't *you* like to see the stars?" Mr. Hao looked at us with pitying wonder. "*Wo i-ching kan hsing,*" he said. "I've already seen the stars." Mr. Hao, whose teeth gleamed in perfect whiteness and regularity, watched us brushing our teeth the first morning and wanted to know what we were doing. "Keeping our teeth clean," one of us replied. "Don't you ever brush your teeth?" Mr. Hao shook his head, perplexed. "*Wo miyu da kung fu,*" he said, "I don't have a lot of time." These two expressions, about the stars already seen and not having a lot of time, have been part of our private vocabulary ever since, taking on a thousand shifting shades and meanings and uses as the years passed.

Ordinarily, our breaks from working routine were trips within bicycling distance, usually out into the countryside to the Western Hills, carrying with us fresh-baked bread from home and wine and cheese from a Trappist monastery not far away, sometimes to temples where we would stay overnight in bare stone rooms and go walking in the cool mornings through the surrounding woods, like the great white birch grove at Wo Fu-ssu, or at the more distant Tan Che-ssu where we would go splashing in the stream that came down over the rocks on the steep hill behind the temple and fell here and there into deep glistening pools.

The idyll was punctured by intruding reality. As I have already mentioned, Liu was arrested as he was leaving Peking and we were quite unable to do anything but be more cautious about close contacts with any Chinese. There were months of work after that, but the apartness of it all had begun to erode the pleasure. In the end, we could no longer remain so isolated, so separated from the real world that was still out there just beyond all these garden paths. We decided to leave not only Peking but China because we no longer wanted to be so visible and so privileged as "foreigners." The Chinese word for "foreigner" is "outsider" and we wanted to return where, for better or worse, we would be "inside." When we left Peking in June 1935, we had put together the collection of short stories in *Straw Sandals,* and I had finished the first draft of *The Tragedy of the Chinese Revolution,* the book I like to think made it impossible for the Stalin version of the history of events in China in the 1920s to stand up under serious scrutiny. That book earned a firm place in the literature on the subject. It also earned me decades of unrelenting hostility among my onetime friends in the Chinese Communist Party, including some I was re-encountering now, not one of whom mentioned the book to me when we met again here this time.

* * *

All of this was passing like film on the screens of our minds as we walked through Ta Yang Yi Ping Hutung again for the first time in forty-five years. It had not changed much, wide enough for a car to pass through if walkers pressed to its gray walls on either side, notched at intervals by gates leading to the living places behind. It was by the gates, indeed, that we were able to recognize our houses, Wilma's by the two stone lions that still stood guard in front of it, ours by the large solid red doors, faded and peeling now, unmistakably the same. But nothing else was. Inside, all was appallingly different. Every square foot of space had been filled with small hovels of rooms made of scrapped bricks, odd pieces of wood and tin. These covered all of what had been the courtyards, leaving only narrow passages for the occupants—five families of some twenty-five people at our house—to pass in and out. At the Fairbanks' house—now occupied by thirty people in seven families—a vestige of the great wisteria vine that overhung their courtyard could still be seen. At our house, we could barely recognize the section that had been our study and bedroom. Its windows were glass, not the translucent paper of our time, a touch of modernization. We could still see a small section of the wall that bounded our main courtyard, where cats used to stroll, contemptuously looking down at our dog Mugwump as she leaped and fell, barking hysterically in what she knew was a safely vain attempt to reach them. People now living in the house received us with courtesy and some curiosity when Wilma told them we had lived where they lived now. We stood as in a ruin, among houses that had survived gracefully for hundreds of years and had now been irretrievably mashed into a jam of hovels. If we could have gone again to the top of the wall, we would not have seen any green carpet of treetops, but we could not, the wall was no longer there. It had been razed to make way for "progress" and much of its debris and broken brick had clearly gone into the hovels that now filled the neighborhood, the space where the wall had stood, and beyond it in a tumbled congestion of slums. It was pollution on the ground fit to go with the pollution that was graying Peking's blue skies and lining the lungs of its vastly more numerous swarms of people. It was from such quarters as these that the crowds we saw came to fill the parks looking for whatever had been left open and green.

We had to hurry back through the hutung and out onto the broad avenues to our hotel. A car was coming to take us to Soong Ching-ling's house for dinner.

SOONG CHING-LING

The high gate opened into a great palace garden, its walks and trees and pond like pictures in the late dusk. From the steps of the big house we were hastily ushered through chilly rooms and halls to where Soong Ching-ling waited for us, seated in a large easy chair in one corner of a huge room at whose center a table was set for a dinner of twelve. From high on the wall, large portraits of Mao Tse-tung and his soon-to-be-displaced successor, Hua Kuo-feng, looked down as a reminder that this was a government building which she now occupied as a vice-chairman of the state, as Sun Yat-sen's widow, as, indeed, a living national treasure herself. Her face still showed her the beauty she once was, her body now grown heavy, her legs useless—she had to be helped to rise, to sit, to move from one place to another, gripped under her armpits and carried as she skimmed her feet across the floor—arthritis, she said, gesturing away her disability with her small hands. I kissed her on the cheek in greeting, realizing as I did so that it was the first time I had ever done that. There had never been more than a handshake to express the real affection we shared in that time past in Shanghai and which reappeared in the bright warmth of her welcome to us now. I slipped back naturally into calling her Suzie, as I did then.

*　*　*

I first met Soong Ching-ling at her home in Shanghai, the Sun Yat-sen house at 29 Rue Moliere in the French Concession, in the fall of 1931. I was brought there by Agnes Smedley as a prize find in her quest for sympathizers with the cause. A willing recruit, I

Soong Ching-ling, Shanghai, 1933

soon plunged into activities—the *China Forum,* the China League for Civil Rights, drafter of statements and press releases—that were for the most part proposed, discussed, planned, and pursued in frequent meetings right there in Soong Ching-ling's living room and at memorable dinners at her table.

I have already remarked that Agnes Smedley aroused skepticism as well as sympathy. Soong Ching-ling produced no such ambivalence. She was, first of all, beautiful, intense in her own much quieter way, and not much less single-minded where her political interests were engaged, but she also communicated a sense of things that was at the same time more rounded and complex and yet simpler and more straightforward. Agnes Smedley seemed to see people as poster-like figures, nearly as cartoon caricatures, often as puppets pulled by the strings of class forces, playing out a harsh morality play in which the "good" were pitted against the "wicked." Soong Ching-ling knew how much more mixed things really were. She had her own kind of skepticism shaped out of her long experience, applied more to individuals than to ideas. She was schooled more in the interaction of people in politics than in the turgid intricacies of ideological "lines" of one sort or another and the conflicts that came sizzling out of them. The broad general direction was enough to determine where her feelings and sympathies lay and for which she was ready to put all her prestige and personal standing to the best possible use.

Soong Ching-ling was a prominent figure in the "Left Kuomintang" in 1927 when Chiang Kai-shek smashed the Kuomintang-Communist alliance and set up his own regime at Nanking. She broke with her family when this split took place. Her younger sister, Mei-ling, married Chiang Kai-shek less than a year after the massacres of 1927. Under this arrangement, Chiang set aside his first wife, and, reportedly, also a second wife, converted to Christianity—he became a Methodist, like the Soongs—and acquired powerful family allies. Soong Ching-ling's older sister, Ai-ling, was the wife of H.H. Kung, a major banker who became a top figure in Chiang's government. Her brother, T.V. Soong, became Chiang's Finance Minister and served him through all the years of his rule. For her part, Soong Ching-ling fled to Moscow after the debacle in 1927, and lived in exile in Berlin. She returned briefly in 1929 to be present at the dedication of the Sun Yat-sen Mausoleum built in Nanking, and again, for good, in 1931, not long before I met her. Through the years she had been close to the Communist Party but she never joined it. She remained an independent figure in her own right, capable of winning support among people who never would or could otherwise move into the Communist orbit. This is what she did as an initiator and leading figure in the struggle against Kuomintang repression and in the anti-Japanese movement of the early 1930s, advancing her causes not just by the power of her name but by the quality of her person and her presence.

Soong Ching-ling's honorific high office in the Communist government after 1949 not only lent it her personal prestige, but served also as part of its nominal non-Communist component. This was made up of a number of aging non-Communist notables whose presence supported in a purely ornamental way the regime's claim to be democratic while they as individuals and as leaders of their various long-defunct organizations conformed dutifully to whatever the Party leadership required of them. Soong Ching-ling focused her energies and interests in these years on child care and education and a variety of social welfare causes. Her role in politics was another far less visible matter. Her personal alignments and connections lay with the older more pragmatic "moderate" elements of the Communist leadership represented by Chou En-lai and not with the more volatile radical figures grouped under the mantle of Mao Tse-tung by Mao's wife, Chiang Ching, who must have been fiercely jealous of Soong Ching-ling's status and prestige. The key fact, I think, is that for all the long duration and depth of Soong Ching-ling's involvement in all this history, she never became a seeker after power for herself. This, more than anything else, enabled her to confront the complexities of all the politics of her years without being diminished by them.

On the other hand, if she ever differed from the Party line or protested acts of repression, she either did so privately or, like so many others, kept her views to herself. I do not know what future study of the available record might turn up, but the whole world would certainly have heard her, in the days of the anti-Rightist campaign of the late 1950s when tens of thousands of writers, teachers, and other intellectuals were purged and exiled, or during the Cultural Revolution a decade later when the numbers of harshly treated victims rose into the millions, had she ever spoken out as freely against injustice and repression in the Communist years as she did so often and so boldly in the Kuomintang years in

Shanghai. She was herself a target of the Cultural Revolution. Though she could not be touched directly—her Shanghai home was raided and vandalized—as far as I have been able to learn she only struck back at the Gang of Four when everyone else did, after their fall. She revealed in one published article that she had been unable to get help or even get to see one of her own old friends and co-workers held prisoner during that time and beaten and harassed until he was driven to commit suicide. About Soong Ching-ling in these years much waits to be learned and to be said. For my part, I feel no need at this point to add to my store of disenchantment but am content to stay down in my time capsule and write of her in these pages only as she appeared to me as I knew her during those years in Shanghai long ago.

In my dealings with her then, Soong Ching-ling was soft and she was hard, she was distant and always correct and cool, yet warm and ready with appreciation of work done and, as time went on, with friendship, affection, and trust. Trust most of all, I think, because she was forever surrounded by people who sought to use her in various ways, especially the Communists and other radicals with whom she was always associated and with whose outlook she generally agreed, but again in general and in the large more often than in the many-shaded particulars. Her experience had taught her to be diffident, reserved, and cautious about those who came to hover around her. No one dominated Soong Ching-ling and she had a way of being crisp, though always gracious and polite, with anyone who gave off the air of seeming or wishing to do so, as in our small circle Agnes Smedley often did.

If this sketch suggests that I was smitten, it is because I was. I was smitten hard by this beautiful great lady, as who could not have been, it seemed to me then, and seems so to me now. If there are no warts on this miniature portrait, it is because I never saw any, and if there were any I was not seeing, I am just as glad. I was twenty-one and, as I have amply indicated, enormously impressionable; she was about forty and enormously impressive as a woman and as a person. For her beauty, her courage, her queenly espousal of just causes, I came to love her like a young knight pure in heart. In return she bestowed on me an ever correct yet warmly personal affection. Make what one might of that now, that is how it was.

The coming of Viola into my life in the midst of this unavoidably touched some of the unacknowledged inwardnesses of this relationship. Soong Ching-ling was utterly gracious toward us as newlyweds, showering us with gifts, welcoming the newcomer to her table of friends at her house. (On one such occasion we paused on our way up to the living room in her house to admire four panels that hung on the stairway wall. Early next morning, to our dismayed astonishment, in came two men carrying those panels. We have them still.) Viola herself was going through a great rush of new experience and exposure. It had to take time before she could enter the warmth of this association and even then, inevitably, it was with a difference that never quite went away. For my part, my young knightly loyalty was now clearly divided, though summoned forth in such different ways in my changing life. I was certainly not young and foolish enough to confuse them. My work in hand, my admiring devotion to Suzie, my love for Viola flourished together in a time of wonderfully consuming commitment. How all this appeared to Suzie herself, I have no idea. On these matters we never exchanged a single word.

Soong Ching-ling's experience of life was shaped by her marriage at twenty-three to a great revolutionary hero who was nearly twice her age. That was in 1915. Sun died in 1925. She became the Widow of Sun Yat-sen and spent the rest of her life living up to the demands of that status. This required that she remain the Widow and forego much she might have had in a freer life of her own. Even if she had not chosen to pursue the politics in which her husband's name remained a great force, this would not have been easy. As it was, she became the target of scurrilous gossip used as a deliberate weapon against her and many friends with whom she became identified in politics during those turbulent years. I remember once, when the latest such bit appeared in what was called the "mosquito press" in Shanghai in the Kuomintang days—anonymously published underground sheets which specialized in gossip for hire and were widely used for both political and private purposes—she said to me in a rueful half-jest: "They've had me in affairs with all these men and I've never had a single moment's pleasure out of any of it!" Many stories and much gossip followed Soong Ching-ling all her days, but unless some believable account turns up hereafter, it seems that truth about this part of her life will disappear too among the myths certain to envelop her after she is gone.

Of my own friendship with her, especially as it touched on how she regarded our mutual Communist friends in Shanghai at that time, I carry a sharp final memory of my own. After my own parting of ways with the Communists came early in 1934 and shortly before Viola and I left for Peking, there was a last time I went to see her at 29 Rue Moliere to say goodbye. Once again she listened as I tried to explain why I had to act as I had and why the work I had done with her and for her had to come to an end. She heard me through, as she had before, with distress and concern. As we parted at her door, her final word was a warning to be careful. I thought she meant to be careful of Kuomintang thuggery. But no, she said, she meant our Communist friends. I looked at her incredulously. "Yes," she repeated, "be careful. You don't really know these people. They are capable of anything."

By the time I saw Soong Ching-ling again, ten years later, the illusions that still underlay that incredulity of mine were long gone, buried with all the dead in Stalin's Russia. I still clung to fainter or more modest hopes about the chances for democratic socialism, but I no longer thought I knew for sure how a more humane human society might come into being, much less be hurried along. Whatever else it was, the war we were in was being fought to keep Hitler and Japan's generals from deciding the future shape of the world, and that at least left open what might come of it after they were defeated. In Chungking, Chiang Kai-shek's wartime capital in West China, where I came as a reporter to cover one of that war's minor theaters, I found Soong Ching-ling working as hard as ever at promoting her chosen causes. The Kuomintang-Communist rift had been thinly papered over by a new "united front" in common pursuit of the war against the Japanese. Soong Ching-ling had accordingly papered over her rift with her family. She now appeared frequently at public occasions with Chiang Kai-shek, only yesterday the bloody-handed oppressor, and his wife, her sister Mei-ling. During that time in 1944 and early 1945, I used to call on Soong Ching-ling whenever I came through Chungking, cordial and friendly meetings always.

Our talk was almost entirely about the tangle of current affairs, the tenuous and fragile triangular relations among the Kuomintang government under Chiang, the Communists represented in Chungking by Chou En-lai, and the Americans under General Joe Stilwell. What Chiang wanted to do was get all the American help he could and husband his forces for a showdown with the Communists. What Stilwell was trying to do, in the face of obvious Kuomintang corruption and ineffectualness, was to make both Chiang's and the Communist forces more immediately useful against the Japanese. What the Communists wanted to do was position themselves to claim power after Japan was defeated. No one was making much headway against the Japanese, but there was no question about who was winning the propaganda war on our side. The Communists were winning friends and influencing people, both Chinese and American, acquiring a reputation for political and military effectiveness by preserving an atmosphere of popular support and heroic austerity in their northwestern bases, carrying on a scattered guerrilla war behind Japanese lines across the northern provinces of occupied China, and scoring with special effect by rescuing and safely returning downed American fliers from that area. In the web of people maneuvering and negotiating these relations at the top in Chungking, Soong Ching-ling played her own unique role. While carrying on her chosen work of relief for war victims, especially children, she also could function as discreet diplomat, contact person, and a giver and getter of information among key individuals on all sides.

For my own part, I looked on all this with sympathy for Joe Stilwell, whose singleminded virtue finally cost him his job, without doubt that the foulness of Chiang's regime assured its downfall, and without danger of being infected—as not a few other Americans around me in Chungking were being infected every day—with new illusions about the Chinese Communists. I could count on my inquiries being received with forthcoming frankness by Stilwell, with bland caution at Chou En-lai's headquarters, and with barely polite hostility at Chiang's ministries. Kuomintang hostility did me in at the end. I was barred from China in the spring of 1945. Only a few years later, with Mao Tsetung triumphantly installed in power in Peking, *all* Americans were barred from China. This lasted a long time, it turned out, and longer for me, as I discovered through Soong Ching-ling, than for others.

During the twenty-two years of severance between America and China that began in 1950, I saw the occasional references to her in the press as a high honorary official of the Communist regime, including the report of the attack on her house in Shanghai during the Cultural Revolution. American-Chinese contacts resumed in 1972. My own first contact with Soong Ching-ling came a year later when I sent her the Introduction to *Straw Sandals* in which I had written about her activities in the Shanghai days. After some time a note came from her, circuitously through my son, himself a correspondent for the *Baltimore Sun* stationed at that time in Hong Kong. The note was a brief comment about *Straw Sandals,* but its real message was in its salutation, which used initials that had been part of our private code of communication during the Shanghai days. During the next few years whenever I let her know that we would be as close as Hong Kong, she tried to invite us to visit her. Once when she had sent word that she would "try to facilitate the visa problem," a wire followed shortly thereafter saying "Doctor forbids receiving friends owing influenza." It was signed "Suzie." I wrote her once from India in 1975 and had no reply until one day early in 1976, a "China Reconstructs" calendar, a promotionally decorative item sent out from China to many people abroad, arrived in our mail at home. Clipped to one of its pages was the sliced-out piece of a letter which I have already mentioned, the note, written by someone in English, that advised her sharply that I was "a traitor" and "never should be invited." By the next time I wrote, in 1980, to say that we were going to be in Japan and would be glad to come for a visit if we were invited, things were different in Peking. Mao was dead, the Gang of Four were gone, and Soong Ching-ling, whose friends were back in power, wrote to say she had passed our letter on with a strong endorsement (she was Vice Chairman of the People's Republic but still needed someone's approval to invite an old friend) and that we would have a reply soon. And so we did. On an evening a few weeks later we were driven to the palace in Peking where Soong Ching-ling lived.

*   *   *

On the way in from the gate, one of her aides warned us that Soong Ching-ling was suffering from a bronchial condition and could not over-use her voice. She had asked us to come for an hour before dinner and even this had been cut, to my chagrin, by a tardy driver. There was much I had hoped to ask her about, even wishfully imagining that she might give me some hours in the next few days to answer questions about her untold story. But if it seemed likely she would not, it soon became clear that she quite possibly could not. In any case, she was obviously going to talk now about what *she* wanted to talk to us about, and that was the little packet of pictures she had ready on the low table before her.

"I want to tell you about my family," she said. The pictures were of two attractive young women, the older Yolande, twenty-three, just married, she said, and the younger Jeannette, twenty, now studying at Trinity College in Hartford, Connecticut. She had informally adopted them when they were babies, she told us, and had raised them as her own. Half their lives had been consumed by the Cultural Revolution which had halted schooling for everyone, even for the adopted daughters of the Vice Chairman of the state. ("I used to go to school every day," Jeannette told us when we visited her later at Trinity, "but there were no classes. We just played.") Yolande, the older girl, became an actress. Her recent marriage had been to a somewhat older man of whom Soong Ching-ling had not, it seemed, greatly approved. "I had someone else in mind," she said. But he was a figure in the theatrical world and Yolande had fallen in love with him, and parental authority was no longer what it used to be in China. Suzie spoke with some annoyance of the fact that Yolande now lived in the city with her husband in a small apartment and not in Soong Ching-ling's palatial mansion where there were rooms to spare. It was a matter of government regulations, she explained. She spoke of Yolande with the pain of maternal loss and of Jeannette with high maternal pride. She had been unwell herself at the time of the wedding and Jeannette had plunged in and taken charge of all the arrangements. As it was, Soong Ching-ling had been unable to remain in the room for the whole of the wedding ceremony and had left for fear of showing how she felt. Having parted long ago from her own sisters and brothers and never having had children of her own, Soong Ching-ling, now old enough to be a great grandmother, had clearly snatched from her circumstances some of what it was like to be a mother.

We told her a little about our children and grandchildren, showed her our pictures. It was a very parental conversation. Viola managed to change the subject when she said: "We think of you every day because of those four panels you gave us. They hang on our wall. They've been with us everywhere we've lived." And

Suzie replied: "It was a good thing I gave them to you! If I hadn't, they would have been destroyed!" It was an allusion to the looting of her Shanghai house and I seized upon it to ask about the rest of her story, had it been, would it be, could it be set down somehow by someone? She waved the question away. No, she had never considered it, would never think of it. An American publisher had offered her half a million dollars for it, she laughed—"imagine, half a million dollars!"—but she had turned him down. That was too bad, I said, she was wrong. If she did not see to the writing of her story, it would be written by others and her own view of herself would be lost forever. Not only would we be left without her version of every major event in China for more than seventy years, but we would never have her own picture of the person who had lived through this long experience. She heard me out, shook her head. "No," she said again, and very plainly closed the subject.

But my question had stirred distant memories not unlinked to the here or now. We were visiting her only a few days after the Double Tenth, the October 10 anniversary of the 1911 revolution which overthrew the Manchu dynasty and made Sun Yat-sen the first president of the Chinese Republic. He was quickly forced out of that office, but he became the revered Father of His Country. In the Kuomintang years, everyone bowed regularly before his portrait and recited his Three People's Principles. His remains lay in the great mausoleum built for him by Chiang Kai-shek in Nanking. In power, the Communists had largely ignored Sun Yat-sen. Under Mao Tse-tung there could not be more than one father of the country. The Communists had their own anniversary to mark the victory of their revolution on October 1. They took no notice of October 10. Sun's portrait never hung among the great ones up on the wall at Tienanmen. No Chinese had any place on the altar of Mao's cult of personality, only, until a short time before our visit, those foreign fathers or grandfathers of the revolution, Marx, Lenin, and Stalin. But it was being reported, we had heard, that the regime would observe October 10, 1981, the seventieth anniversary of the 1911 revolution, and it seemed quite likely that a portrait of Sun would go up on the wall on that occasion alongside or near Mao's, now hanging there by itself. This would neatly serve several purposes; it would be a gesture of accommodation toward Taiwan, do greater justice to history and at the same time serve the new leadership's wish to deflate the single figure of Mao, "to demote him," as someone said, "from holiness." Soong Ching-ling said nothing of all this, but she unexpectedly began to talk about her girlhood in the pre-1911 days when her father Charles Soong, a Christian minister turned entrepreneur, used a printing press he had established in Shanghai to print Bibles and Christian tracts to print leaflets instead for Sun Yat-sen's party, the *Tung Men Hui,* as the Kuomintang was originally called. Sun's achievement was not sufficiently recognized now, she complained. "After all," she said, "to bring down an empire was no small thing."

I could hear other guests arriving in the anteroom. Two or three people I did not know had already come in and were politely standing apart while we talked. I found there were words I still wanted to say to her, if this was to be my only chance. I said I had come to know in all the years since Shanghai that the politics of power had little to do in the end with the visions of human betterment with which we all began, that all the political questions keep on being asked and the chances of decent answers keep on getting lost along the way. "But I want to tell you, Suzie," I plunged on, "the one thing I do carry with me as precious from that time in Shanghai was the love I had for you." Soong Ching-ling looked at me with a face I could not read. She half-closed her eyes and in her soft hoarse voice said, "I am honored."

Ting Ling came into the room just then and came right over to us, no polite standing apart for her. They met with a great embrace. It had the air of being their first meeting in a long time. A few minutes later Mao Tun came in, walking slowly with a cane, eighty-four years old now, almost sightless, fragile. After he and Soong Ching-ling exchanged a similarly emotional greeting, we exchanged ours. They were the two figures from our past that I had particularly mentioned in my letter to Soong Ching-ling that I hoped to see after seeing her. Other guests arrived, General Stilwell's two daughters, women in their sixties, a famous Buddhist poet named Chao Pu-chu, and others who appeared to be members of her own immediate staff. I was seated at Suzie's right. When I remarked that the best food we had ever eaten in China had been at her table, her face broke into a sudden pleased smile. She told me her old cook and housekeeper from the Shanghai time, a very sick old lady now living out her time here in this great house, had remembered me when she was told I was to be here this evening. Tell her, I said, that this food is good but not as good as it was when she cooked it. Dinner done, the short evening came to an end. I asked if another hour or two might be possible. She said she would let me know.

But there was to be no more time with her, I was sorry to learn, and I could only tell myself that she *was* fragile, unwell, and very old, and that there were still ceremonial demands that she continued to insist on meeting—the French president was coming in the next few days and she was to appear at several functions. In any case, it was clear enough that she could not or would not talk with me more about the times past, her role, her feelings about herself. A few days later, with a packet of magazines to deliver to Jeannette when we saw her, came a note. It was written with the same bold strong strokes done with a snub-nosed pen that I first saw in the first note she ever wrote to me more than fifty years ago. "Have been delayed with work," it said. "I am afraid we have to go to Outer Space for our next encounter."

Postscript:

Soong Ching-ling died in Peking on May 29, 1981, age ninety. While she lay on her deathbed, she was made a member of the Communist Party and was named Honorary President of the People's Republic. The Communist leadership seized upon the occasion of the death of Sun Yat-sen's widow to make a major propaganda pitch at Sun Yat-sen's political heirs on the island of Taiwan, where the Kuomintang still rules a "Republic of China" headed by Chiang Kai-shek's son, Chiang Ching-kuo. The Peking government invited Taiwan's leaders and Chiang Kai-shek's widow—Soong Ching-ling's sister Mei-ling—and all members of the Soong family and of Sun Yat-sen's to attend the funeral. Chiang Ching-kuo* and Mrs. Chiang Kai-shek, who lives in the

*The Communist regime's effort to woo Chiang Ching-kuo into returning Taiwan to their national fold has gone to the length of the virtual rehabilitation of Chiang Kai-shek. On his own road to power in 1927, Chiang broke out of the first "united front" with the Communists, slaughtered them by the thousands, and became the prime symbol of the oppressive system the Communists were trying to overthrow. On their own road to overthrowing Chiang, the Communists in 1936 entered a second "united front" with Chiang to pursue the war against Japan. In their accounts of this history, Chiang was characterized as a "bandit" and a "running dog" of the imperialists. But now, according to a *Washington Post* report from Chiang's birthplace in

United States, spurned the invitation, as did apparently the surviving Soongs. The "relatives" who did come to be photographed at her bier were "grandchildren" who were not her grandchildren at all but Sun Yat-sen's by his son, Sun Fo, his only child by an earlier marriage, and other even more distant members of the Sun family with whom Soong Ching-ling had never had any connection at all.

It happened that I had a call from the *New York Times* the day Soong Ching-ling died to ask me for any information they might include in their obituary. I told them about her two adopted daughters Yolande and Jeannette who had become her children when she was close to seventy and whom she had raised as the only family she ever had. This information was included in the *Times'* account the next day. In following weeks, I was astonished to discover that these two young women appeared in none of the photographs taken of family and friends at the funeral. There was no mention of them in any of the obituary tributes and accounts of her life that filled Peking publications which we received. I have not been able to discover any credible explanation of why this was so. I can testify, however, how harshly this violated Soong Ching-ling's closest personal concerns and I can only imagine how sad and painful this must have been for the two young women for whom, as she made plain to us when we saw her, she cared most in the world.

On October 10, 1981, the Communist regime in Peking did take notice for the first time of this date in modern Chinese revolutionary history, and a large portrait of Sun Yat-sen did appear on the wall at Tienanmen next to the portrait of Mao.

The sketch here of our own re-encounter with Soong Ching-ling and my recollections of her in Shanghai fifty years ago was completed just before her death. I have left it intact as it was written.

October 15

Fong Mu, a well-known critic and editor of the journal *Wen Yi*

Chekiang: "...The old Chiang mansion has been restored and the tombs of Chiang's closest relatives have been rebuilt." Chiang, a local official explained, "is a historical figure. Our dispute with him is a problem left by history. Now we must bury the differences . . . and reunite the motherland."—*Boston Globe,* January 8, 1984.

Pao, or *Literary Gazette,* came to the hotel to pay what appeared to be an official welcoming call. A robust-looking sixty, Fong Mu had the air of being the man in charge. When he finished his rather formal greeting and we sat down and poured tea, I asked him how we came to be invited.

"I don't know about the past," he said, "but we are now ready to invite all friends of China and especially friends of Chinese writers. It has been a long and difficult period. It is not strange that we should hear so many things about you. Why, we even heard unhappy things about Agnes Smedley, Anna Louise Strong, and Edgar Snow, negative things!" I winced at being located in this company of long-faithful fellow-travelers, at having my "negative things" lumped with their "negative things," and being welcomed back like a prodigal, returning from a much greater distance and a much longer time away from the fold.* "The world is too big," Fong Mu went on, "and things are too complicated. China was isolated for a long time so there is difficulty for Chinese in understanding the world. With this visit, let this be a new beginning between us."

It was easy to imagine Chou En-lai speaking these same words to Kissinger/Nixon and Teng Hsiao-ping saying them again to Carter during the process of resumption of Chinese-American contact after so many years of separation. And lesser Chinese officials similarly welcoming all sorts of visitors for whom, with the disappearance of Mao and his Gang of Four, resumption of contact with China had become possible, all the way down to these two visitors with their somewhat unusual strands of connection to a bit of the Chinese Communist past. In this, as in much else in our talk, Fong Mu faithfully echoed the new leadership in Peking which was trying to bring things down from the extravagant ultra-radical flights of the Mao era back to that solid good Chinese earth which, they knew, was so much more favorably familiar to Westerners, especially Americans.

---

*Agnes Smedley (1894-1950), mentioned earlier in these pages, and Anna Louise Strong (1885-1970) were writers who spent most of their adult lives as faithful followers in Stalin's camp, coming each only in her last years to unhappy final outcomes and disenchantment. Edgar Snow, who did his journalistic fellow-traveling around an orbit somewhat more distant than the other two from the hardcore center, stayed faithful in his fashion until his death in 1972.

Our conversation moved quickly to the larger context of current affairs—the problem of "judging Mao," of freedom for writers—and I did not try to bring it back to the personal level, partly because I was diffident, possibly too diffident, about staying at that personal level, but also because I was interested in those large affairs and this was a first chance to hear something about them from a man in Fong Mu's position. The result was that in a long morning's talk I did not learn any more about what my hosts knew or thought they knew about their guest, but I did get a view of what a Party veteran of sixty had to say about things going on in post-Mao China.

(This turned out to have even more particular interest because in this encounter I first came on what I grew to see was a meaningful difference between those in their sixties, like Fong Mu, and those in their seventies-eighties, like others I met. I will bring all these observations together in one place later on in these notes.)

OCTOBER 15

TING LING

When Ting Ling was kidnapped by Kuomintang agents in Shanghai in 1933, she was thirty years old, a well-known young writer who had just joined the Communist Party. In later years she became one of the leading figures and a combative fighter in the ideological and factional battles that went on in the Party's cultural establishment in the years just before and after the Communist victory in 1949. Ting Ling had less than eight years of life in the open under the Communist regime she had so ardently helped to create. In 1957 she fell victim to Mao's Anti-Rightist Campaign which purged a whole generation of writers and intellectuals from the Party's ranks. She and her husband, Chen Ming, a poet and scenarist, spent the next twelve years on a labor farm in Heilungkiang in northern Manchuria, working first at raising pigs and eventually as teachers. In 1970, during the Cultural Revolution, they were separated and sent to prison where they remained, uncharged and untried, for five years. They were released in 1975 during Teng Hsiao-ping's brief return to the capital, only to be seized again when Chiang Ching and her cohorts regained the upper hand. This time they were sent to a labor farm in Shansi where they were kept for more than three years, finally returning to Peking and rehabilitation in 1979. During this whole time her published works were banned, her unpublished manuscripts disappeared, her name was not mentioned. Ting Ling spoke of her twenty-two years in limbo in tones of blunted anger. "We all suffered during the Cultural Revolution," she said, adding with a harsh laugh: "Those who did not suffer would change places now with those who did!"

We talked of her experience during a morning's visit at her

Ting Ling, Shanghai, 1933

apartment, a simply furnished place of four or five small rooms in one of the large new apartment houses that now line Changan Tajieh, Peking's main downtown thoroughfare. It was modest by any middle class standard elsewhere but positively luxurious here where even a little private space is a privilege that goes with the factional draw in the non-stop game of political and bureaucratic power at every level in the Communist system. From being among the last for so long, she and her husband were now belatedly sharing some of the advantages enjoyed by the first in the small handful of favored few in the land. With us was her husband Chen Ming, a quiet man some years her junior, hair still black, devoted, attentive at her side. Ting Ling answered my questions in a strong, expressive voice. Her manner, like her stocky solid frame, belied her seventy-seven years and her frail health. Her candor, I thought, covered much she left unsaid.

I asked her what had happened after her kidnapping in Shanghai in 1933. Her prolonged disappearance had led first to rumors that she had been killed and then to whispers that she was "cooperating" in some manner with her captors, a charge that was revived decades later when she came under attack by Party opponents. I heard from her now that she had been kept prisoner in Nanking not in a prison but unofficially in a house maintained by Chiang Kai-shek's secret police. She was held there for three years, until late in 1936. In the beginning especially, she was put under heavy pressure to write an article for publication in Shanghai to show that she was not dead. What her Kuomintang captors wanted from her most of all was something that would look like evidence that she had defected to their side, as so many of her fellow Communists were doing at that time. They also wanted to still the clamor raised by her disappearance among surviving "legal" liberals in Shanghai, including this young editor in the *Forum,* and amplified abroad by sympathizing writers and intellectuals mobilized for protest in such cases by the Comintern apparatus. In the end, it appeared, her captors lost interest in her. In late 1936 events were moving toward the new anti-Japanese "united front" between the Kuomintang and the Communists. Surveillance lightened and one day she simply walked away, making her way to Shansi first and eventually to Yenan, the Communist stronghold in Shensi. There she joined the Communist literary establishment and was soon embroiled in what became a long struggle over the role of literature and writers in the revolution.

Ting Ling lost the husband of her youth to the Kuomintang terror. The newborn baby son of that marriage was sent to be raised by Ting Ling's mother in Hunan while she continued on her own revolutionary course. But these heavy losses aside, there are ironic comparisons that can be drawn between what she suffered under the Kuomintang and what befell her thereafter at the hands of her own Communist comrades. The Kuomintang confined her for three years, her Communist comrades put her away for more than twenty-one years. In the first case, she remained a person, the writer Ting Ling, and voices could be heard from as nearby as Shanghai continuing to demand to know what had happened to her. In the Communist limbo in which she spent the best decades of her maturity, Ting Ling remained a non-person throughout to all in her world, except to those with whom she labored on the farm and the jailers of the prison where she was held. Her Kuomintang captors pressed her to write something, anything, to make her existence known. Her Communist captors swept her books off all bookshelves, seized her manuscripts, including a novel and hundreds of thousands of words of a diary, she told us, work she never recovered. In a much quoted speech she made in the first flush of her return to life and rehabilitation at the end of 1979, Ting Ling herself pointedly drew this parallel by her use of pronouns. "In the 1930s," she said, "the Kuomintang banned my books. After 1958 we ourselves banned my books . . ." And her son, the martyred Hu Yeh-pin's son, deprived of a father by the Kuomintang, caught some of the lash of the fate met by his mother under the rule of the Communists. "He went to the Soviet Union in 1953," Ting Ling told us, "to study how to build submarines. By the time he came back in 1959, I was already a 'bourgeois Rightist,' a 'counter-revolutionary,' so he was not allowed to go into submarine work. He was relegated to another kind of less important construction work in the military."

In Ting Ling's talk of her experience, there run notes of some bitterly won wisdom, of despair, of caution, all hidden under frail formulas about the "Revolution" and "feudalist thinking" and, perhaps most of all, a stubborn romanticism filled with illusions about the "goodness of the people" and about herself. Ting Ling's essential picture of herself, from her girlhood until now, is of a perennial rebel, always at odds with authority but always moving with, not against, the revolutionary stream. This stream may sometimes pause in eddying pools, at other times is a rushing torrent rising in high crests and falling in deep troughs, but it moves on always and one must always move with it, at whatever cost. Even at seventy-seven, Ting Ling, survivor of more troughs than crests, could still talk this way, although, almost soundlessly, one could also hear the themes of loss, of anger, of waning energies sapped by time and age and now by gnawing illness; Ting Ling came back from limbo just in time to undergo an operation for cancer.

"This is a long history," she said, "of more than fifty years. The Chinese revolution is a long story of difficulties and zigzags. I was always in front of the big wave, and I got splashed. When I was only ten, I fought feudalism. Then I took a long roundabout road, and now we must still fight to do away with feudalism. Chu Chiu-pai [a noted Communist leader of the 1920s-30s who was attacked and ousted by his comrades and was executed in 1935 by Chiang Kai-shek] once described me with a proverb about a moth flying into a lantern. The revolution is on fire, I fly into it, then out, and in again, and at last I must die in the fire. I am still like the moth and will seek truth in the fire to my last day. One truth is that the young now are not as they were in the old days. And we are not as we were when we were young. At that time we were simple-minded, the revolution was simple and sacred, we carried our heads high, we threw ourselves into it. After Chiang Kai-shek fell, I thought the revolution was won. Now after long experience, we have suffered, we have moved ahead, suffered again, and now we know better.

"Things are now more complicated, more difficult. To destroy is easy, to build is difficult, especially to deal with a kind of thinking that has lasted a thousand years, feudalist thinking. I think that if great numbers of people take part in it, it is the right way. I know one thing surely, the old saying that if a person is put in a difficult place, he has to do his best to struggle his way through it.

"Maybe I have a narrow view, maybe I am narrow-minded. I suffered a great deal for many years, under the Kuomintang in prison, under the Communists in prison again, my books forbidden, then allowed, then later forbidden again. Many people cursed me and spread rumors about me. But I still think ordinary people are good. I like ordinary people. I concede there are a lot of bad

Ting Ling, Peking, 1980

things in China. But there is a lot of hope too. I stay optimistic. I see a bright future. But how to eliminate suffering of this kind? Why did it have to take place? One can't avoid mistakes, even the Party can't. But twenty million people suffering and dying? I don't know. On my farm out there eleven people died."

And this was all just a "mistake"? Yes, she insisted firmly. "The most serious thing is that there is a feudalist problem in Chinese minds. I mean that people are not well educated. We are trying to change this. Before only one person could speak out, others could not speak. They wanted to worship some one, it makes things simple that way when there is one person to worship. We have to draw lessons from this, great heavy lessons."

Thus Ting Ling on Mao, leaving his name cautiously unspoken, critical of some of what was past, careful about the present, wishful about the future, but also, it now appeared, through with it all as far as her writing was concerned. When I asked her what she was writing now, she said she was working on a long novel about peasants, and about peasants, moreover, in a pre-revolutionary setting. "About peasants?" I asked incredulously. "Yes," she replied, "I know peasants, after all I lived all these years with peasants!" But how about her own story, I asked, what was she going to do with the material of her own life? She waved the question away with her hand. Her own story was not the important thing, she said. Was that so, I said. Books about peasants were a dime a dozen, I went on, she had already written several, one had even won a Stalin prize, but was not likely to be remembered for long. "You have the chance to write *the* book," I pressed on, "by which this whole period's experience will be remembered. Do you really mean you are not even going to try?" Ting Ling looked at me through those tired eyes, clearly taken aback by my sudden vehemence. "I have written some short essays about my own experience," she said rather lamely. (She presented me that morning with a copy of her slender little book of short sketches about herself about which I have since gathered enough to know that it does not begin to touch the essence of her story.) She looked at me with pain, I thought. *Could* she write a book now that the whole world would read in years to come? I did not know whether I was reading this question in her face or hearing it in my own mind.

I must add that on the subject of Ting Ling's writing, I stand on uncertain ground. She said that morning that she had not written very much, "only about twenty pieces of work," she said. Very little of it has appeared in translation and what I know of it is secondhand. My own most vivid impression of her as a writer goes back to the story that won her fame in her youth, "The Diary of Miss Sophia," which she wrote in the mid-1920s before she committed herself to the Communist movement. She was then one of the vibrant and passionate young romantics breaking away from what they saw as a hideous past and reaching for new experience, new vision, and in that particular story, the new experience of love. Not long afterward Ting Ling followed her young husband into the maelstrom of revolutionary politics and she brought that same vibrant and rebellious passion to the quest for the new experience of "revolution." This led her down quite other paths as a writer; one can doubt that her attempts to produce what was called "revolutionary literature" assured her any immortality. The new experience did lead her, however, first as a disciple of the late great writer Lu Hsun and then as a literary bureaucrat herself, into bitter intra-Party struggles over what that literature was supposed to be and what writers were supposed to do.

"The main work is writing," Ting Ling said now, pulling back from the sharp edge our conversation had reached. "In our times a Lu Hsun appeared. Another Lu Hsun will appear. Many great people appear in the struggle. I will write anything I want to write. Sometimes I write something I don't like. But I have to be loyal to myself, not to tell lies, to speak from an inner voice, from the bottom of my heart. Otherwise I would be afraid of writing anything. You gradually get used to criticism by others. I don't care now about others' criticism. Literary works must be tested by time. Real writers will not be beaten down by criticism."

"Yes," intervened her husband Chen Ming at this point, "but you were beaten down for twenty and more years." Ting Ling looked around at him. "Yes," she said, "but I am like the wild grass. After the wind passes, it stands up again."

Could she now write anything she liked? "It is hard to say," she replied. "Some work gets a lot of interference, some less. In revolution some people would rather be left than right. 'It is lovely to be left,' they would say. Now, right now, there are no officially appointed controls. You are allowed to have arguments. There are no very clear limits now."

Chen Ming spoke up again. "In the past it would not be said in so many words, write the bright side, not the dark. But if you did write the dark, they'd say you are anti-Party. What they need to know is that brightness and darkness are two sides of the same thing."

Ting Ling and Chen Ming paid us the considerable compliment of coming to see us again, at our hotel this time, for a farewell visit before we left. She wanted to tell me, she said, that she *would* write about her own life, but not until she finished her work in progress about peasants.

October 16

Chien Men, the gate in the southern wall of the old city through which we used to bike on our way to the Temple of Heaven, stands by itself now, a wall gate without a wall, a great ungainly torso with jagged stumps like crudely severed limbs protruding on both sides, remnants of the wall that used to stretch away east and west in its aged and massive bulk and grandness. When they cleared what is now the vast square open for half a mile in front of Tienanmen, the main gate to the Forbidden City, Chien Men was left standing at its far southern end, like a partly destroyed tomb still housing the ghosts of a forgotten past.

We drove past it bound on another small sentimental journey to the Temple of Heaven, in our minds the most memorable of all the old places in Peking. It is a circular building with a roof of blue tile, rising in the center of a large park at the top of a long march of steps flanked on both sides by spacious pavilions with roofs of golden yellow tile. When we used to come here, as we often did, it was the highest point anywhere around the city under the great clear blue Peking sky. It is no longer the highest point and the sky is no longer clear or blue. Now from much of the surrounding arc of gray horizon rise the blotches made by ugly Russian-style buildings. Back of them, cranes and chimneys reach like random black marks into the bleak and smoky sky, the shapes of more of the new world a-coming. In the temple pavilions on either side of the wide stone plaza just below the Temple of Heaven itself, there are now shops, souvenir shops, with big painted signs outside to advertise their "antiques" for sale to tourists. The one on the left, hard to believe, announced itself as The Marco Polo Antique Shop.

Along the walks in the park, loudspeakers hung from lamp

posts were loudly bleating forth what we were told was part of an old Chinese classic tale. Until recently they had given forth an incessant blast of propaganda. In the new less strident post-Gang of Four dispensation, stories were being told instead, with intermittent messages enjoining people not to spit or drop litter. It was not possible, it seemed, to leave the air to the sounds of the strolling crowds and playing children. It was not a scene in which to recapture moments past. It was awash with people, large groups of foreign tourists in guided parties, and everywhere in the park the usual great crowds of school children and people taking their leisure in the open. Still, standing in the stone plaza in the crush, the din of the loudspeakers reaching us like the sound of crows screeching nearby, we got some help. As we looked up at the temple, the gray sky broke and a jagged piece of the old bright blue opened above us and we could look at the temple's dark blue crown against it, as we had always seen it when we came here in those times before.

We walked back along one of the stone paths that radiate from the temple like spokes of a huge wheel to gates in the park wall. We used to picnic here under these trees, on cheese and wine and fruit and cake. Two old ladies walking toward us suddenly stopped when they came close and the older one, a doughty-looking woman with thinning gray hair and a brown lined face, thrust a pointing figure at Viola and asked: "How old are you?" "I'm seventy," Viola replied. The old lady put her finger on her nose. "I'm eighty," she said, her companion was seventy-two. They protested in disbelief, Viola could not possibly be seventy. This began a conversation which quickly gathered a listening crowd around us. I asked the lady of eighty how she compared life now to life as it was before. She exploded into an altogether spontaneous and voluble endorsement of everything that had happened to her. Her husband was a retired postal worker, her son was in the postal service now, her clothes were better, she said, plucking at her sturdy cotton blouse, so was the food she ate, her children's schooling, driving each point home with a flailing arm and outpointed finger. It was the strongest testimonial to the regime we heard on the whole journey.

*   *   *

Another sentimental journey took us to Wo Fo Ssu, the Temple of the Sleeping Buddha, out past the Summer Palace up the slopes of the Western Hills where we used to go on our bicycles, sometimes staying the night to walk in the early morning through the surrounding woods. That quiet and tranquil scene was now a noisy and crowded tourist attraction, jammed with family groups, lines of school children, and on this day a contingent of teenage naval cadets, boys and girls in neat blue uniforms, all together filling the courtyards, filing through the temple pavilions, gazing up curiously at the ancient figure massively reclining in the main hall. We wandered through, the busy scene swirling around us. We stopped for a bowl of soup at an untidy refreshment alcove and watched the crowd go by, sighing a little for what was beyond recapture, marveling a little at how this small monument to ancient superstition—part of the "feudal" tradition so vigorously rejected by good Marxist-Leninists—now served as a showplace for the masses. There was no touch of reverence in the procession of visitors here now, but then there never was much that a westerner would call "reverence" in the way Chinese have always dealt with their many kinds and levels of religion.

We tried to go on to Tan Che-ssu, that more distant temple, higher in the hills, bounded on its wooded slopes by rock-filled streams with crystal-like deep pools where we used to peel and splash and gambol and laugh. But on the way at a guardpost on the road, we were stopped by a sign that read: "No Foreigners Allowed Beyond This Point," with a soldier posted there to enforce it. Our hosts, Li Shin and Ho Pin, argued first with the soldier, then with his captain, summoned from some nearby billet, but to no avail. Why was such a place out of bounds? It was being rebuilt, we were told. Perhaps the villages beyond here were not as visibly improved as those nearer the capital city, perhaps some part of Peking's air raid defense system was located here, not to be seen by spying foreign eyes. Or maybe the temple *was* being refurbished. Whatever the case, there was no breaching the barrier. It was of course higher and more impassable than those polite guards standing in the way. Whatever was going on at Tan Che-ssu now, repair or decay or anti-aircraft guns on the hillside, it was surely no more available for naked splashing in mountain pools than we were, now.

MAO TUN

When I first met Mao Tun in Shanghai, he was a slight, quiet, alert man of thirty-six who always accompanied Lu Hsun whenever he came to our house. On these visits, Mao Tun acted as Lu Hsun's interpreter. Fifteen years younger than Lu Hsun, he was already foremost among the younger writers thanks to what is still his best-known novel, *Midnight,* a picture of life in Kuomintang Shanghai, and short stories like his *Spring Silkworm* and *Autumn Harvest,* both of which appeared in translation in the *China Forum.* His work, unlike much else written at the time, was marked by its faithfully careful portrayal of his social settings but even more by his creation of characters who were more than mere poster-like actors in the drama of the class struggle. Mao Tun was an active figure in the group around Lu Hsun, in the writers' league they formed, in publishing journals, and in helping younger writers in the difficult and dangerous half-legal half-illegal lives they all led in Shanghai in those years.

We found Mao Tun, now a frail man of eighty-four, in one of the larger old-style houses that had not been demolished or hovelized but remained a spacious place with a wide courtyard, its surrounding apartments apparently occupied by members of his family. Dressed not like everyone else in a Mao uniform but in an old-fashioned Chinese long gown and jacket, he walked out with careful steps to greet us and ushered us into an austerely simple but comfortable reception room where we had our brief talk. He had forgotten all his English, he said, with an apologetic wave of his hand, though he plainly understood my questions and occasionally corrected Ho Pin's translation of his replies. Mao Tun is now honorary chairman of the Writers Association and holds other

Mao Tun, Shanghai, 1934

honorific posts but obviously could not be very active in any of them. Our Writers Association hosts had warned us we would find him hard of hearing. It is not hard to imagine that he might have turned a deaf ear to some of them, but they would not have had much occasion to discover it, for we found on meeting him that he could hear well enough, it was his eyesight that was failing. We also quickly learned that though he might not see very clearly, there was nothing unclear or clumsy about the way he skirted hard places in our talk. And there were hard places enough in his story.

In those early Shanghai years, the young Mao Tun was an important figure not only because he was an unusually gifted writer but also because he was a veteran member of the Communist Party which Lu Hsun had never joined but to which Mao Tun had belonged since its beginning in 1921. The tension between his two roles, gifted writer and Party cadre, imposed itself on his whole subsequent career. Partly perhaps because of Lu Hsun's influence and partly because he was so gifted, he could feel the pull of the writer's autonomy and the view of literature as an expression of the many-sidedness of human experience. But as a Party man who accepted the sanctions of ideological orthodoxy and discipline, he always yielded in the end to the contrary idea of literature as a tool of politics and the writer as a soldier in the service of the Party's cause. Since the "Party" meant the "Party line" in all its shifting and wriggling varieties and since it also meant power-seeking bureaucrats in the cultural domain in all *their* shifting and wriggling kinds, Mao Tun, like all writers in China in these years, led a difficult existence. His creative work as a writer seems to have come to an end even before the Communist Party came to power in 1949. In the first years of the regime, he became Minister of Culture and appeared in varying and often ambiguous roles in the incessant and bitter factional and interpersonal conflicts among writers, artists, and bureaucrats. Never firm enough in behalf of his writer-impulses and never tough enough in the infighting among the cultural commissars, Mao Tun finally fell from his slippery path into limbo. He was dismissed as Minister of Culture in 1965 and disappeared from public view, as did his books from public shelves. He did not reappear until 1977, after the fall of the Gang of Four. This whole time, all the turbulent years of the Cultural Revolution, he now told us, he spent right here in this house, safe under the personal protection of Chou En-lai.

When I asked him to tell me about this experience, he began by reciting his political biography, from the beginning in 1921 and his work as a propagandist and political officer in the army during the revolutionary movement of 1924-27. It was a tempting subject for me to stay with, but our time was limited. I nudged him forward to 1949 when he went to Peking and became an official of the new regime. Here again, he dwelt at length on the push-and-pull among contending persons and factions that finally resulted in his becoming Minister of Culture, but slid quickly past his removal from that post in 1965. "I had been there too long," he said, "I was not capable of remaining minister." During the Cultural Revolution, he was not personally attacked. "Red Guards did come to my house one time," he said, "but Chou En-lai protected me. He ordered them to leave. I lived for a time at the Ministry of Culture but was soon able to come back here to my house.'' And there he remained in almost total seclusion for twelve years. I told him how I had sent him a copy of *Straw Sandals* in 1974 only to have it returned stamped ''Addressee Unknown.'' He just smiled and said mildly: ''No letters from abroad were delivered to me during that time.'' He continued to be paid the salary attached to the last job he held as ''vice-secretary of the United Front Committee'' and this is what he lived on. ''I was lucky,'' he said, ''unlike other people, I was not put in the stable.'' To be ''put in the stable'' meant to be sent out to a farm labor camp. ''I was here all the time.''

How did he spend the time? ''I never went out,'' he replied. ''I spent my days here reading Chinese classics.'' What did you write, I asked. ''I did not write,'' came his answer. ''I felt that I had nothing to write about. During the Gang of Four period there was nothing worth writing.'' Nothing, I asked, he had written nothing all that time? ''No, nothing,'' he said. ''The Gang of Four kept watch on me. I had only a few visits from close friends.'' There was a pause full of silence. He broke it. ''You know, there is a Chinese proverb, 'In order to protect oneself, it is sometimes wise to do nothing.''' He paused again. ''All writers stopped writing at that time,'' he added. ''Even many who were not in prison did no writing.''

How did he feel about what was going on? ''I did not know at first that the Gang of Four persecuted so many people. I just knew some had been sent to prison. I did not know that many died.'' Did he see it as a counter-revolution? ''No, I didn't think it was counter-revolution. I thought it was sponsored by Mao Tse-tung but that it went too far. Only after the Gang of Four fell did I learn that so many died during the Cultural Revolution. Chairman Mao sponsored the Cultural Revolution. He was afraid the Party was becoming revisionist. We could understand this, but it was not necessary to go about that way, to attack people for 'taking the capitalist road.' He could have called conferences, had discussion, not sponsored a mass movement, things like the Red Guard attacking the Communist Municipal Office in Shanghai. The Red Guards came to Beijing, he received them, he reviewed them as they marched by, thousands and thousands of them, and he went to a reception for them in the Hall of the People.'' Approaching what were apparently the outer limits of what anyone could say at this juncture in the Party's affairs, he added: ''We need democracy in the Party, democracy in China. In Mao's time there was no democracy, in the Party or outside of it."

But then when I went on to ask where the new limits were located for writers, he replied: "Writers can write what they wish, but counter-revolutionary writing cannot be allowed." What kind of writing was counter-revolutionary writing? This question began an exchange that turns up confused in my notes because it was confused in fact. "I mean anti-Party writing," he said. He explained that he meant "anti-socialist writing" and this meant being against the Party and against the building of socialism. Who would decide what these code words meant? "The masses," he replied, "if the masses think a book is not anti-Party, then it isn't." It would "be up to the masses to decide." The "masses," of course, meant the Party which of course represented the masses. Such decisions had to be made by responsible Party officials. "People are very sensitive right now," he offered in response to my request for an example, "they are writing letters to the newspapers. Decisions about publishing such letters must depend on the attitude of the writer. In principle everything is allowed, but you have to check the attitude. A story about bad things that happened, that's all right. If somebody criticizes the

With Mao Tun, Peking, 1980

Party for bad things that have happened, that's all right too. But if someone wants to expose shortcomings of the system, then it is bad.''

What would Lu Hsun think of this? Mao Tun's reply was categoric. ''Lu Hsun would not allow any counter-revolutionary anti-Party writing.'' This picture of Lu Hsun as a man of power who would ''allow'' or ''not allow'' this or that kind of writing hung there in the air for a long moment, an unconscionable caricature that could only be drawn by people who needed to recast Lu Hsun in their own image. In this brief encounter with this sad and feeble old man, I could no more enter into challenging argument than I could hope, by the most patient and persistent questioning, to draw out more of what he felt and thought about all that had happened to him and his Revolution. He was standing fast behind his protective wall and whatever he actually thought or felt about his life was hidden there. His failing eyes stood additional guard against intrusion. Without eyes to meet, I found, there was almost no expression to read. There was only what was said or left unsaid to go by. Mao Tun did not show even a flicker of anger about his own years of isolation or the harsher fate met by so many others. But this was not the time or place nor I the person to try to pierce his defenses. I asked him what he was writing now and his answer was consistent. ''I am writing my autobiography,'' he said. ''It will cover from my youth to 1949.'' And the time since? ''When I finish that much, if I still have time,'' he said, ''I will write about after the Liberation.''

At this point, the allotted hour had given out. A photographer entered the room and pictures were taken. With his slow step, Mao Tun accompanied us out to the courtyard where we said our goodbyes.

*   *   *

Postscript: Six months later, Mao Tun's time gave out. He died in Peking on April 5, 1981.

October 17

In search of the more positive side of things, we went, at Viola's request, to a primary school that was available for foreign visitors, the Second School of Yu An Street. Here the children, obviously accustomed to such visits, chanted "Welcome" in English and applauded at all the right times without cues. The school building was spotless, classrooms in impeccable order. The children sat stiffly upright with their hands clasped behind their backs, raised hands in a uniform manner to answer questions, applauded each recitation by one of their number. It was a scene of total control, the bright-faced children flawlessly following an exact script, the teachers, careful and earnest, conducting their performance.

There were some 1,200 students in this school, first to sixth grade, and at least half of them were out on the great open playground when we came out of the building. The top three grades were having their recess in what certainly looked like a romping contrast to the snap-to-order regime of the classrooms. Here the restraints were off. All around us colorfully dressed children were running, tumbling, playing games, chasing each other, wrestling, shouting, laughing, a picture book scene of happy children at play. We stood in a small group at one side with the principal and several of his aides. Had I not been facing the field looking at the children as we chatted, I could not have seen what happened when a teacher dressed in a gym suit, standing on a raised platform, blew a single piercing blast on a whistle. In what I have to insist was less than the flicker of an eyelid, those swarming children, 600 or more of them, swept out of their jumble into a dozen or more instant lines, straight lines, I mean West Point straight lines, beginning right in front of us and streaking back, at least fifty of them in each ramrod aisle, to the wall at the far rear of the field. Free as the free play had seemed to be up to only a few seconds before, it was clearly all taking place within a few feet of each one's assigned place, that each squad or group had its moments of free play within a prescribed space so that they could, at the signal, leap in a split second into their places in their assigned rank and order. At the head of each section, now standing at rigid attention, were group leaders with three-stripe insignia on their sleeves, each one wearing the red kerchief of the Young Pioneers knotted around his or her neck. These were the sergeants and corporals of this oncoming guard, chosen to take this first rung up the ladder to Partyhood for their special adeptness, perhaps their display of swift obedience, or possibly, like all the children in this school, also because of the status of their families.

What followed was an extended mass drill display executed with Rockette-like precision by these nine-to-twelve-year-olds, some of it like calisthenics, some of it in the dance-like movements of *tai-chi,* some of it smartly military, all of it together a spectacle of extraordinary discipline, order, and control, the teacher whistling or sometimes barking out his orders from the platform, the whole ensemble responding like a machine. At one point, a pert little girl of about twelve took the teacher's place and gave the orders. At another, the commands came from a tape played through the loudspeaker system, a nationally used tape, it was explained, that made this drill a uniform exercise everywhere. It was quite a performance, like pictures of similar displays in Russia and Eastern Europe and in Hitler's Germany, and sometimes on a smaller scale on American football fields at half time. Here was the schooled innocence of children casting ahead of them images of docile masses of order-takers, with the underside image that surfaced in 1966 when the Cultural Revolution began, the explosion of Red Guard violence, the controlled suddenly turned loose, licensed to run amok.

The show in the schoolyard ended. In long double lines, the children filed back into the building to resume classes. As we walked back ourselves, we saw to one side a class of first graders, twenty or so little ones of six, getting their first drill in snapping to orders. Another young man in a gym suit was teaching them, alternately murmuring soft and gentle persuasions and barking out orders, teaching them how to obey swiftly and in unison, stretching out their small arms, bending their small bodies, stepping out with their small feet, all together by the numbers, the young instructor now gently drawing this one back who had stepped too far, now lowering the hand raised too high, bending over with easy smiling words and kind hands, then snapping out his next order like the pop of a gun, watching with a pleased smile the two rows of small ones do it better the next time.

LIU TSUN-CHI

We used to call him "Liu Erh"—the second Liu—to distinguish him from "Liu-I"—the first Liu—another friend with the same surname. We first met in Peking on a summer day in 1933 only a short time after he had come out of a Kuomintang prison there. Our rendezvous was at the railway station from which we followed him out to a place where we could talk. Viola and I always remembered him on that day as a tall figure in a gray gown and topped by a straw hat. Perhaps it was because our way led through a scraggly field of high waving grass through which he strode a few hundred feet ahead of us, only his head and shoulders in view. We were all of an age then, twenty-two, and he already spoke the fluent English that proved to be a principal asset in his later career.

I saw Liu again in Chungking in 1944 where he turned up as chief of the Chinese staff of OWI, the American Office of War Information. We met there from time to time during those war days when politics in Chungking, as I have already described them, were such a mix of interests and biases, when some members of the American military and political establishment felt kindlier toward the puritanically upright Communists, as they saw them, than toward the hopelessly corrupt and ineffectual Kuomintang government and army with whom we were officially allied, while others did not care how corrupt or ineffectual our SOBs were so long as they were firmly ours. There was ambiguity and anomaly at every level and every point of the political spectrum of those days and our friend Liu no doubt shared in it in his own way as he faithfully carried out his appointed tasks. In 1947 he came to New York on a mission to buy printing equipment. I had seen his two small children in Chungking, now he saw ours. He returned to China and some years later, in the not-so-puritanical pit-like arenas of internal Chinese Communist politics after the Chinese Communist victory, Liu, we heard, was accused of having been an "American spy" during the war years. We heard no more of him after that. Like so many others, Liu simply disappeared from view.

Back in Peking on this journey of re-encounter, we asked about him, wondering whether he were alive or dead. We discovered he was indeed alive, was right there in Peking, and, like so many others, was freshly back from years in limbo. His voice turned up on the telephone, full of the same welcome surprise we felt at this chance to meet again. In our minds Liu was still the slender, straight, dark-haired man we had last seen, until he stood in the doorway of our room in the Beijing [Peking] Hotel, not as tall as we had thought him to be, but about my own height, not slender but still straight, with a head of white hair, clear eyes, and a face less marked by the years than my own. A warm gleam of pleasure passed among the three of us as we quickly exchanged notes on how we happened to be there, how we came to discover him, what he was doing now—editing a new encyclopedia in a new publishing house, he said—and he even asked me, what about *you,* what has been happening to *you* all these years? Later, I said to that, we wanted to hear first what his story had been since we had last met.

In Peking in 1949 after the Communist regime was installed, Liu was a member of the journalists' delegation to the Consultative Conference for the Constitution. He became head of the China Information Bureau and later of the Foreign Languages Press, which published *People's China,* the *Peking Review,* and other materials in English. He set up the foreign section of the Hsin Hua News Agency. In 1957 he fell victim to the "Anti-Rightist Campaign," a massive purge of writers and intellectuals from the ranks of the Communist Party. This was the forerunner of the even greater and much bloodier purges of the so-called "Cultural Revolution" that began in 1966. Liu was among the earliest of the millions of victims swallowed up in these sweeping attacks on most if not all the literate members of the Party.

He was sent to a labor camp in northern Manchuria. Ting Ling and Ai Ching, a leading poet, worked on a pig farm nearby. After several years there he was sent to exile in Hunan, in central China, and then to prison, remaining in one form of limbo or another until 1978, the twenty-one best years of his life. Now seventy, restored to Party membership, rehabilitated, exonerated of all charges brought against him, Liu was trying to retrieve some sense of being useful, which he said was now the most important thing, and his faith, which he said was intact.

During the long years of his exclusion, Liu carried with him the label of "Rightist." This was quite literally a label, attached to his personal record, if not actually worn on his person, the identification that fixed his personal status. Every individual in the Communist system carries a label that determines the conditions of his life, such as Party member, worker, peasant, government official, as of this or that class origin, and this or that place in the myriads of Party, government, and working hierarchies. Vast numbers of purge victims carried the tag "Rightist" or other disabling labels with them for years. Even after political change at the top brought them back from limbo to life, it took a lengthy process of re-examination before the Party that had given this or that label finally took it away.

Liu's journeys as a "Rightist" were long and painful. His stay at the Manchurian labor camp lasted two and a half years, through the bitter starvation time of the Great Leap Forward in 1958-60, another of Mao's inspirations that was supposed to result in a great spurt of production but instead brought the country to the edge of famine and disaster. "I was finally unable to walk, during that hard winter of 1960," Liu said. "But I did survive. Many died." In one of the many convulsive Party zigzags of that time, Liu and some other "Rightists" were brought back to work in the crippled government, but their labels were not removed. After periods of illness and intermittent work as "an eleventh grade translator"—"there were many lower grades than that," he explained with a smile—Liu was sent to exile in a small town in Hunan. He was supposed to work there as a teacher, but found no job, only confusion, closed schools, hungry people, and local officials who did not know what to do. He was finally sent to a nearby state farm to work as "librarian." There was not much to do. "My other job was to ring the bell for lunch and at quitting time." Liu spent his days at a table in his library and translated English books he found moldering on the shelves. One of his translations, he said, with a slightly twisted smile, Sir Walter Scott's *Ivanhoe,* had actually been published in Peking since his return. Liu sat out this stultifying exile as the months stretched into years. When the

Cultural Revolution began in 1966, he was ordered to join in the marches and demonstrations that took place every day for a while. Everything else stopped. "I didn't even have to ring the bell anymore," he said. His time of wasting went on, stretched by now to more than ten years, until one day in May 1968 he was arrested.

"They came for me and put handcuffs on me," Liu said. He held up his hands, fists clenched, face taut, eyes clouded, and held them there for a long few seconds, lowering them finally into his lap. "For two weeks, day and night, I was interrogated by a five man group, one of them in uniform. Three were about thirty, two over forty. I was then fifty-seven years old." Then, handcuffed, he was taken by train for the long trip back to the capital where he was put in a single cell. "So I was in prison again, in Beijing in 1968, as I had been in 1931, in solitary confinement."

He paused, then went on: "When I was in the Kuomintang prison that first time, I felt proud and confident. But now I was in the People's Prison, in the *People's* prison. When they came for me"—he held up his wrists again—"they handcuffed me, *handcuffed* me, I was depressed, so depressed, I nearly cried. But I couldn't cry, I didn't cry, I didn't want them to see me cry." He held his hands in the air before him some seconds more before bringing them down again. "And my crime now was not just that I was a Rightist, but also a traitor, a renegade. I was arrested in 1968 and charged with having been a renegade in 1933."

"I was in that prison in Beijing," Liu went on, "from the middle of May 1968 until December 10, 1969. I was given newspapers to read but was allowed no visitors, no letters. Food was brought to me in my cell. I could speak to no one, hear no one. Even the jailer who brought me my food made me lower my voice to a whisper when I asked for anything. I was clearly not supposed to be heard by any other prisoners or to hear them. All were under the same rule. I could hear nothing, nothing. I tried to listen for sound, any sound at all. There was a hole in the ceiling and a window, high above my reach. But no sound, no sounds even of birds outside.

"On December 10, they came and put handcuffs on me again." He held up his wrists once more and the anger came up in his voice and in his eyes. It seemed to be the memory of the handcuffing that could break through his otherwise controlled calm. "I was taken from Beijing by train again to a prison in Changsha, in Hunan, a so-called Detention House operated by the Cultural

Revolution Committee. There I stayed from December 1969 to July 1970. I was not isolated in this place, the cells were for two or four prisoners, mostly politicals. But by this time I was ill and weak and I thought I would die soon. I wrote a letter to the prison authorities asking to be given some light work in the yard so that I could get some sunshine. Instead, not long afterward, I was sent to a prison on an island in Tungting Lake at Yuenling, a prison for long-term prisoners. Conditions there were much better. It was a proper jail, in fact, it was the No. 1 prison in Hunan, a regular prison run by regular judicial authorities with professional jailers. I could do some work, twisting rope on a rope-making machine. Then I was given a job as an agitprop (agitation/propaganda) worker. I edited a wallpaper in which prisoners could write, expressing regret for their crimes, mostly murders. There were very few political prisoners in this place. I stayed in that prison for five years. I never heard anything about any trial or sentence on the charges against me.''

* * *

Liu was arrested in 1968 on charges of having been a traitor and renegade in the 1930s. This was a familiar feature of Communist factional demonology. In Stalin's purge trials, old Bolsheviks were accused of having been spies and traitors not just recently but in all their years back to the beginning. And so it was too in Mao's China in the time of the Cultural Revolution when the attacks on Party veterans were frequently justified by charges that they had been traitors, Kuomintang agents, or imperialist spies decades before, in the 1930s. This was made easier to do by the fact that during those years there were many so-called ''recantations'' by Communist prisoners in Kuomintang jails. These were often quite genuine. Not a few ex-Communists earned their freedom by joining Kuomintang police to hunt down and arrest former comrades. Many of these statements, however, were fabricated by the Kuomintang authorities to sow whatever doubt and confusion they could among their Communist foes. Out of this history, the Communist Party inquisitors who succeeded the Kuomintang inquisitors were able to trump up charges against almost any Party veteran who had been in Kuomintang prisons or worked in the Communist underground of that time. Indeed, such veterans were often the particular targets of Mao's wife, Chiang Ching, and her cohorts who badly needed to bolster their own legitimacy as newly come leaders of the Party.

In Liu's case, he was charged with having won his own release from prison in Peking in 1933 by signing such a recantation, and of being involved in another more famous such episode three years later. In the first instance, in 1933, there actually was a statement issued by the Kuomintang headquarters in Peking with the names of fourteen prisoners, including Liu's. By that time, however, Liu had already been released as a result of quite other circumstances and in these, I now heard for the first time, I unexpectedly turned out to have played a contributing role. Liu reminded me that I had published in the *China Forum* a letter from that prison in Peking detailing the conditions in which political prisoners were kept there. Liu was the author of that letter whose original text was signed with several names, including his own. In response to that letter, a delegation of the China League for Civil Rights went to visit the prison. Its leader was Yang Chien—murdered in Shanghai only a few weeks later—who noticed Liu's name on his cell door and called it to the attention of another member of the group, a well-known Peking liberal, Wang Chuo-jan. Wang brought to bear his personal connections with higher officials (personal links, again, being the crucial element in all Chinese politics, Kuomintang then or Communist now) and as a result of his plea for Liu as "guilty only of youthful patriotism," Liu was released. "So you see," smiled Liu, "I really owed my freedom in the first place to the *China Forum*!"

But the story of Liu's debt to Wang Chuo-jan was not done. Thirty-five years later, in 1968, when Liu was in prison and charged with being a renegade who had won his release from prison in 1933 by signing a recantation, word of his plight reached Wang Chuo-jan. Wang had become one of the non-Party members of the Communist State Council. In 1968, he lay old and ill in his home when he heard of the charges against Liu. He sat up all one night, Liu learned later, writing a statement explaining how Liu had actually gotten his release from prison at that time. He died twenty days later. But that document, "eleven pages long, written in large characters," eventually served to clear Liu's name of that particular charge. "So twice in my life," Liu said, "I benefited from this man's benevolent spirit."

The second charge laid against Liu rose out of a more complicated episode in 1936 involving a "genuine" statement that was actually faked by the Communist prisoners themselves to get out of prison and back to work for the Party. This was the famous or infamous "Case of the Sixty-One" which acquired a special importance at the summits of Chinese Communist politics because it involved no one less than Liu Shao-chi, who, as already noted, was long regarded as Mao's successor but was denounced as chief of the "capitalist roaders" and died as Mao's prisoner in 1969. He has since been posthumously rehabilitated and restored to a place of honor in the Communist pantheon which is obviously not a very restful resting place. In 1936 Liu Shao-chi was head of the North China Bureau of the Communist Party. At the end of that year, Chiang Kai-shek was forced by a rival warlord—this was the "Sian Incident" in which Chiang was "kidnapped" and released only when he accepted terms the Communists helped to dictate—to declare an internal truce and accept a "united front" of all groups and armies in China to fight the Japanese. Mao and his forces were then in far-off Shensi. In Kuomintang-controlled territory, the Communist movement had been decimated by government repression. Liu Shao-chi desperately needed experienced cadres to enable the Party to seize the opportunity offered by the new situation. He instructed the sixty-one prisoners in the Peking jail to sign a statement saying that they were leaving the Party, to win their release thereby and get back to their Party work. And so they did and were released and all but two of them did in fact return to Party activity. Several became prominent leaders in the struggle that ended in Communist power twelve years later. One of them is a vice-premier today in the government dominated by Teng Hsiao-ping. Liu Erh's role in this famous high level affair was a humble one. He had been in that prison, he knew the channels of communication in and out of it, and he helped the messenger who got Liu Shao-chi's instructions to the men inside. When he was arrested in 1968, he was accused, along with all of them, of having been a traitor. It took nearly ten years and a major turnaround in the Communist Party leadership to bring about the exoneration of Liu Shao-chi and along with him all the others who shared in that episode, including our friend Liu Erh.

Liu was in his seventh year in prison in Hunan, still without trial, when one day in 1975, he heard that Teng Hsiao-ping had returned to a position of power in Peking as vice-premier. Teng was there only briefly before being sent back to limbo again, but during that time, he put through a decision in the Military Commission to review all cases of detention and to release those against whom crimes had not been proved. The results reached Liu some time afterward when a provincial security officer, a batch of documents in his hand, abruptly told him: "You will be released. You will resume work. Your pay arrears will be given to you."

This matter of pay, incidentally, was an interesting feature of the system. As illustrated in Liu's case, the wage he was earning as a government official when he was purged in 1957 was 220 yuan a month, or 129 U.S. dollars at the current official exchange. When he was sent to the labor camp in Manchuria and later into exile into Hunan, he received the downgraded stipend of 76 yuan a month on which he had to maintain himself. When he was put in prison in 1968, this stipend stopped. What they paid him as arrears upon his release was the 76 yuan a month for all the months of his seven years in prison, less 11 yuan a month to cover the cost of the food he ate as a prisoner. "What I received," he said with a sour smile, "was just over 5,000 yuan!"

Liu was freed from prison but not from exile and he was still a "Rightist." "This label was still on my personal file, which was with me. The work I was supposed to resume was that job as 'librarian.' But that administration no longer existed, I found. I was handed over to a new agricultural department where I was told to go to the new Agricultural College at Changsha to work there, to do something, anything, even to rest for a time if I wished. I was still a 'Rightist.' At Changsha I became a librarian again, and there I stayed until the end of 1977. Then I was suddenly called to the Hunan Provincial Party Committee and told that the Academy of Social Science had appointed me to a post and I was to report for work at the end of February. So I returned to Beijing, still a 'Rightist' and still earning 76 yuan a month."

It took all the rest of the year 1978 to go through the process of rectification and rehabilitation. It took several months just to remove the "Rightist" label. Liu was appointed second in charge of a new publishing house with responsibility for editing the new edition of the China Encyclopedia already under preparation. His name was put on a priority list of those going through the correction procedure in the Party's Organization Department. Even so,

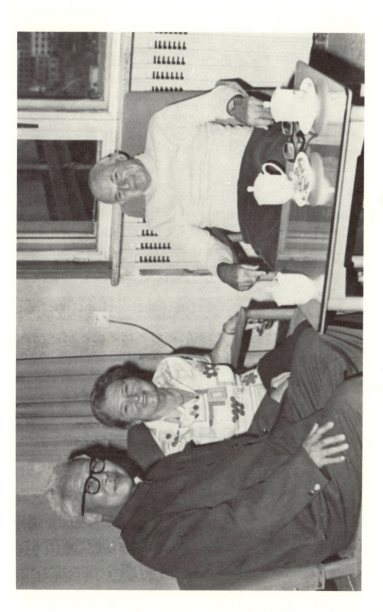

With Liu Tsun-chi, Peking, 1980

it was not until nearly the end of the year that formal decisions were finally handed down in his case. He was cleared of all charges, restored to membership in the Party. "By December 1978," he said, "all the wrongs done to me were corrected. I was finally back to where I was before the Anti-Rightist campaign began in 1957." He added wryly: "I was back to my old status, back to my old salary of 220 yuan a month." All that was missing was twenty-one years of his life.

There was a silence in the room until I finally asked: "How did you feel, how did you feel about what happened to you?" There was another pause, and then he replied: "How do you suppose I felt? It is hard to put into words. Many people like me have died since 1957. Many, many people, many more since the Cultural Revolution began in 1966. When I came back to Beijing I tried to find old friends and acquaintances. I found that among those I knew, more had died than were still alive." Liu was saying, in unspoken answer to my unspoken thought, yes, he had lost much of his life but he was still alive, he had survived, and even this was hard to say.

*   *   *

No one seems to know how many died in China's Cultural Revolution. The lowest figure for deaths I heard was half a million, but other estimates ran to millions. Many died from starvation and illness, many more by suicide, which was encouraged by interrogators and jailers. In detention centers and prisons and in the wild rampages of the youthful Red Guards turned loose on their elders by orders from Mao himself, many victims were beaten to death. Finally there were those who were executed. Teng Hsiao-ping himself has estimated that 29 million were victims of this disastrous infliction, including the dead, the exiled, the imprisoned, and those reduced from skilled and professional work to the lowest levels of manual labor. There appeared to be no way of counting the many millions affected as relatives of those victimized, all who suffered deprivation and discrimination, all those pressed into fearful submission and silence. Liu was not sure how to compare this Chinese experience to the purges in Stalin's Russia.

The hard questions hovered, not quite bluntly asked. Where

did survivors like Liu strike their balances between bitterness and faith? How fragile were their defenses against the pain and loss of this experience, these mocking outcomes of youthful devotion and waste of their best years? When I touched on this glancingly, Liu said: "In the days when I was in prison I almost lost heart. I was so disheartened, I didn't want to think of the future. I did compare myself to the victims of the Stalinist purges. But even then, even then"—almost visibly summoning back his reserves—"I felt that some political turn would come, some great change would have to happen.

"I kept remembering that three times in my life I came back from abroad when the fate of the country was uncertain. I was a reporter in Tokyo in 1936 and 1937. The day after the Marco Polo Bridge incident [the beginning in July 1937 of the all-out Japanese attack on North China], I slipped out of Japan and returned to Shanghai. In January 1942 I was in Singapore, I escaped and made my way back to China through Burma. In 1948 I came back to China from the United States. I never lost my confidence in China's ability to become one of the leading countries of the world. I never lost heart or the will to do my part. I could have stayed abroad. There were many chances, then and since. But it was repugnant to me to become an emigre. Long ago I saw the White Russians in Tientsin. I could never be like one of them.

"What weighs on my mind now is not my suffering of the past twenty years so much as our present situation now. What happened in the past is compensated for by what is happening now. There is so much to do, if only there is the energy to do it! I have confidence in the present leadership, it is correct, it is rectifying. Yes, I think there will be more democracy. You have to visualize the almost insurmountable difficulties in the way of our building a more satisfactory society. We are in a very big turn from the past. The prospects are opening now. There will be very bitter struggles in the future."

This wishfully hopeful note I would hear again among survivors like Liu, confidence in the new "line" and the new leadership. There was a sound of defensive caution in it—limbo was always there, perhaps around the next turn—and of gratitude. But most of all there was a sense of a clear and desperate need to justify the faith they had barely managed to keep, to stay alive, to be there, to win this utterly providential second chance to count as individuals, to reach again for the vision that had come to them when they were young. The "lessons" of the experience were going to take a lot of learning; everyone was saying that the democracy claimed by the system had to become more real than rhetorical. The promise of the Communist past on this score was hardly encouraging. Liu, for his part, had a reflection of his own. "Reflecting about it," he said, "I think they were right in 1957 to call me a 'Rightist.' I had enough of a heritage of bourgeois democratic thinking to be called so. I was strongly against the subjectivist dogmatic orders from above about public information and educational work. There were too few rights for those who did the work and did not agree with the dogmatic instructions. I wanted more freedom. So in a way, I *was* a 'Rightist.' They were wrong to call me that, as they meant it, but I *was* on a different track.

"Of course I can never forget the suffering and shame I was put to in the whole course of things since 1957," he went on, "but I don't think it must weigh too heavily on me when there is so much useful work to do. I don't think it was avoidable." Not avoidable? Liu thought for a moment before answering. "I used to stand up there in the days before 1957, up on Tienanmen with Mao Tse-tung on anniversary days. The cries of 'Long live Mao Tse-tung!' were very moving. My children were out there, joining in the shouts. But when it quieted down, I could not see it as a good omen. The old man was thinking too much about himself. He was too far removed, too venerated. You couldn't really analyze it too well."

*   *   *

Liu had four children out there in that mesmerized crowd venerating Mao in those early days. They all figured, as I now learned, in still another chapter of his story of the life of a Communist in China. His children were "all right," he said, explaining that luckily all were old enough to have gone on through higher education before the Cultural Revolution brought education of any kind to a halt for everyone. This made them too old to be seen as members of the post-revolutionary generation—his son became a Party member in 1950 and his youngest daughter is now thirty-eight—though all were heavily affected by what happened to their father in these years. They were all the children of his first wife, the comrade of his youth. Indeed, she was pregnant when she was arrested and imprisoned with him in Peking in 1931 and bore their son in that prison. She eventually became a middle school principal. "We were a happy family," Liu said, "they were good children, we all loved each other." But then their mother died, in 1954. Two years later, Liu married a woman who was also a Party member, so much so, in fact, that when he was expelled from the Party as a "Rightist" barely a year after their marriage, she divorced him. Because of the father's expulsion from the Party, the son, a pilot in the air force, was grounded and shifted to a training job. His daughters, two of them qualified teachers, were refused regular job assignments and lived precariously under the shadow of his blighted status through all the years "until my case was corrected." But when Liu returned from limbo to resume his existence, hoping also to resume a full family life—there were nine grandchildren by this time—he ran into unexpected trouble.

When the Party took him back after twenty-one years of divorce, his wife of that time expected to do likewise. As a "humble tool of the Party"—her phrase for herself, Liu said—she had survived the years without trouble. Although she had cut off contact with his children during all that time, she now sought them out and enlisted their support for a remarriage. But Liu had other ideas. Not long after his return, he married a widowed primary school teacher. "She was low in place, in rank, in education, whereas my former wife was a Party member," and for this reason, apparently, his children opposed the marriage. "They refused to accept her as my wife." They joined with his former wife in this, forcing him to enter upon a new struggle with his children on the one hand and his Party branch on the other. He had to have the Party's approval of his marriage before it could be registered and this was withheld by his branch because of his children's strenuous opposition to it.

"Their attitudes are difficult for me to grasp," Liu said. "My wife is not a Party member. She was seen as having a 'bad origin,' even though I got it officially certified in writing that her father was a vegetable seller in Shanghai, a toiler, with no bad record. Still my Party branch opposed the marriage saying I wouldn't be happy if my family was so upset about it. They advised me to cancel it. But I fought it out with them as a political issue. I appealed to the higher Party secretary, arguing that they were violating Party law by interfering with my private life. He agreed with me and issued an order to my branch to stop its interference. The branch obeyed and gave its approval. By that time I had been with my new wife nearly a year." Winning over his children was taking longer.

Liu shook his head in not-really-mock dismay at his experience. "I have always thought of myself as a conciliatory person," he said. "I don't know why I have had so many conflicts. In my own family, my father had a temper and even as a child I grew up to be a mediator in the family, a conciliator, even between my father and mother. How come in my own life I fight so strongly against my opponents?"

October 18

We went to see Mao Tse-tung in his mausoleum on Tienanmen Square. Instructed to be in place precisely at 8:40 A.M., we arrived to find a long line of Chinese pilgrims waiting on one side and a special place for foreigners on the other. When our Writers Association car brought us there at the appointed time, we found ourselves first in the foreigners' line. Buses were already unloading tourist parties that fell in behind us. Attendants briskly marshalled us by fours. A few minutes later, the Chinese line which had been inching slowly forward was stopped and we privileged foreign devils turned in ahead of the Chinese faithful and moved into the mausoleum hall, dividing into two lanes, filing around the sides of the inner chamber where the body lay in its box on its bier, a pink face above the gray tunic. We caught a glimpse from twelve feet or so away, then moved on at quickened pace to the back door on the far side and out. It was a ritual of worship of a body turned into an idol, one of the more peculiarly obnoxious Chinese borrowings from the Russians. Chinese emperors were put away out of sight in their tombs. But Mao, it was being said, might not lie here alone much longer. The "de-Maoification" process already underway with the bringing down of statues and portraits might include, we heard, bringing in the remains of other leaders of the Revolution to lie with him, re-establishing collective leadership among the dead as well as among the living in the post-cultural revolutionary order of things.*

I asked to see the library at Peida, Peking National University, where I spent many hours in that time long ago. It was then within easy biking distance from our house. But that library was no more, we now learned. The old Peida buildings had been taken over for other government purposes and the university had been moved from its central location to the campus of what used to be Yenching University out at the northwestern corner of the city. A huge statue of Mao Tse-tung, the kind now gradually being taken down by the new regime, stood in the main courtyard. At the library we were greeted by a small aged man who introduced himself as Keng Chi-an, who had served Peida as a librarian all his adult life after studies in the United States. He showed us around the library, now moderately populated with students. During the Cultural Revolution, he told us, it had remained open, but empty. No one ever came. Only he came every day to preside over the silence, like a keeper of the tomb where higher education had been buried in a deep swoon that lasted for ten years. Wakened at last by Mao's septuagenarian successors, it had risen not pristinely beautiful but emaciated and starved and was obviously going to need a long period of nurture and renewal before it could recover from its ordeal.

*   *   *

At the foreign-language bookstore downtown, the shelves were filled with the works of Marx, Lenin, Stalin, and Mao. On the English-language literature shelf were Thoreau, Tennyson, Walt Whitman, Kipling's *Just So Stories,* and Booker T. Washington's *Up From Slavery*. A small crowd of young people pressed against the counter peering up at these books. One of them next to us

*In December 1983, on the eve of an official observance of Mao's ninetieth birthday, it was announced in Peking that the Mao Mausoleum had been "enriched" by newly installed exhibits commemorating three other major figures of the Revolution, Chou En-lai, Chu Teh, the military leader of the "Chu-Mao" armies that became the basis of Communist survival after the debacle of 1927, and Liu Shao-chi, the Communist leader who had long been assumed to be Mao's successor but who died as Mao's prisoner in 1969.

asked in his limited English which book he should choose to read. That depended on what he was interested in, we said. History. Then the best choice up there was Booker T. Washington, we said, and explained to him—and a surrounding group of interested young listeners—who Booker T. Washington was and the historical setting of his story. We could have no idea how much he took in, but the young man did ask for the book.

ABOUT
LU HSUN

We were visited at the hotel by a group of Lu Hsun specialists led by Ko Pao-chuang and Tang Tao, whom we had first met at the dinner the day we arrived. Ko presented me with a copy of a journal with two of his recent articles about Lu Hsun, one of them devoted to the letters Lu Hsun sent to me in 1934 about the selection of stories to appear in *Straw Sandals.* Tang Tao, who used to read contraband copies of the *China Forum* in the Shanghai post office, held out to me a book of his essays open to a photograph—of which more later—of a group in the garden of Soong Ching-ling's house in Shanghai on a day in 1933 when George Bernard Shaw came to visit. There I was, a young man with dark hair, looking over Soong Ching-ling's shoulder, a step or so away from the small figure of Lu Hsun.

Our visitors were evidently workers in the sizeable industry that has grown up around the collection and study of materials of whatever kind relating to Lu Hsun, China's foremost writer of this century. There are Lu Hsun museums and institutes in Peking and Shanghai and research and writing about Lu Hsun has become a major cultural/literary enterprise of the regime. During the Cultural Revolution, Lu Hsun's works disappeared, along with most others, but have since begun to be re-issued. His status as the regime's principal literary icon has been re-established and during our visit we heard much about the elaborate plans being made to celebrate the 100th anniversary of his birth.

Lu Hsun, born in 1881, died in 1936 when he was only fifty-five years old. His fame rests on the works he produced as the first modern writer to produce literature in the *pai-hua,* the vernacular tongue, instead of *wen-li,* classical Chinese, and to do so in a new

Lu Hsun, Shanghai, 1934

medium, the modern short story. All his stories and his equally famous short critical essays, which he also developed into his own uniquely distinct form, were aimed at breaking the crust of oppressive traditions and their modern counterparts as they appeared both in the large events and the individual lives about which he wrote. He was the most important and influential writer of his time in China. He spent his last years helping, organizing, and protecting younger writers caught up in the political turmoil and the pressures of Kuomintang repression and Communist demands on their roles as writers, an issue on which Lu Hsun always sharply differed with his Communist friends and would-be mentors.

At the time of his death in 1936, Lu Hsun was at bitterly angry odds with the Communists, whose general cause he supported but whose need to impose their will on writers he could not accept. Safely dead, his independent spirit and sharply ironical and satirical style were interred with his bones. He was soon beatified by Mao Tse-tung himself, who called Lu Hsun "an unprecedented hero . . . the most correct, the bravest, the firmest, the most loyal, and most zealous hero . . ." But Mao also warned young writers against trying to follow in Lu Hsun's footsteps by adopting his way of dealing with the society around him. His approach was no longer necessary, Mao explained, now that democracy was flourishing under Communist rule. It has been Lu Hsun's fate to be revered like one of the plaster gods he helped to pull down in his lifetime, a figure bearing no resemblance to the man he was. Ever since his death, Lu Hsun's political views have been subjected to agonizingly scholastic examination or turgid ideological interpretation and his ideas about the relation between politics and literature twisted beyond recognition. What he wrote and did has been used and abused by faction fighters on all sides of the many fierce struggles for power fought out between and among writers and Party bureaucrats on the Chinese Communist cultural front. Had he lived, there could be little doubt he would have emerged from the earliest of these battles not a saint but a victim. As it is, it is much easier to imagine Lu Hsun's quizzically scornful reaction to his own canonization than it is to expect any of the work now being done about him to illuminate the reality of this unique and remarkable man.

The group that came to see us at the hotel did not want to talk about any of these matters. They only wanted to check out some items in Lu Hsun's diary in which our names appeared. This diary was obviously not a work of description or reflection but was more like a daily log he kept to record what he had done, where he had been, whom he had seen each day. Since Lu Hsun had come a number of times to our apartment in the Embankment Building, several times for dinner, each occasion was duly noted. One such entry included the fact that there had been eight guests. Our Lu Hsun data collectors wanted to know who the other guests were. Another note recorded that at one such dinner at our house, he met Paul Vaillant-Couturier, editor of the Paris Communist daily *L'Humanite,* who was in Shanghai to attend the "anti-war congress" described earlier. Vaillant came to dinner that night with a copy of one of his books to present to Lu Hsun. What Lu Hsun brought to present to Vaillant was a copy of one of Vaillant's books in Chinese translation. Vaillant-Couturier was an inordinately vain and pompous man, big in body as well as ego. The contrast between him and Lu Hsun was great enough without this added display by Lu Hsun of Chinese-style modesty. Obviously presenting one's book as a gift has some grace in it as well as vanity—on another occasion Lu Hsun signed a book of his to give to me—but I confess that the memory of that exchange between Lu Hsun and Vaillant-Couturier has quivered somewhere at the back of my mind every time in the years since that I have given a copy of one of my books to anyone.

The questioners who came to see me now about Lu Hsun seemed interested only in trivial details, most of which I could not supply. They did not ask what kind of man he seemed to me to be, or what he might ever have said to me that I could add to their record. I do not know that I could have answered such questions usefully. Conversations at those dinners at our house or occasions at Soong Ching-ling's were almost always focused on current affairs, work in hand, or else were kept light in deliberate attempts to relax, something we managed to do sometimes, or even over-do. The print of Lu Hsun left on my mind by these exposures is of a man whose modest manner never implied an absence of vanity, which he had in good measure, but very much after his own particular fashion. One took him to be a man who knew his own strengths and confronted his own weaknesses and who felt no need to impress others with his importance. In his critical and polemical writing, Lu Hsun's style was sometimes sharp and light, sometimes blunt and heavy, but in his bearing toward others, as I ever saw him, he was always modest and courteous, a small quiet man looking on and listening with the quizzical questioning quality that seemed built into his strong face and heavy-browed eyes.

It was I, however, who learned from these questioners today something I had forgotten, though the fact that I had forgotten astonishes me now. One such item indicated that not only did Lu Hsun visit us at our home but that I went to see him at his; that was a time of many comings and goings and perhaps it is reasonable of me not to have remembered this. But far more arrestingly, I was reminded by another one of his diary jottings that on the eve of our departure for Peking from Shanghai at the end of March, 1934, Lu Hsun gave a farewell dinner in my honor, on March 25, attended by ten others, not named. What makes this small fact remarkable is the light it casts on the kind of man Lu Hsun was. By that time, as I have already recounted, I had broken sharply with our mutual Communist friends and they with me. That meant breaking off all personal relations as well. But Lu Hsun, close as he was to the Communists in Shanghai at that time, was not turned away from how he felt about the *China Forum,* perhaps even about me, which was enough for him to pay me the signal compliment and courtesy of such a dinner. That I did not remember this speaks perhaps to the high stress and pressure I was under in those days. Perhaps more likely, I did not yet fully appreciate how demonstrative a gesture it was; what looked like a simple friendly act was in fact a political and personal act of considerable weight. It was also, I must add, an expression of confidence in the completion of the task we had undertaken together to assemble a collection of translated short stories, beginning with those already published in the *China Forum.* Lu Hsun and Mao Tun continued their correspondence with me through the spring of 1934, as I have already indicated, until we finished work on what eventually became the book *Straw Sandals.* Lu Hsun attached importance to that work and was not to be deflected from it and neither was I.

There is already a great volume of writing about Lu Hsun and there will surely be much more to come out of all the work now underway about him in China. But given the heavy constraints imposed by past and present Chinese Communist politics, this work is likely to continue to be mainly hagiographic and unilluminating and, on the subject of his differences with the Party, incomplete or inaccurate. Lu Hsun's own works and especially his voluminous correspondence have only begun to get closer and more searching examination abroad by inquirers who will be seeking to learn more not only about his place in the history of his years but also about what kind of man he was, the sources and meanings of his angers and depressions and their reflection in both his creative life and his personal history. The freedom needed for inquiry of this kind is not available under the present regime in China, any more than it was in the past.

* * *

Lu Hsun's son had asked to come to see us. He appeared at the appointed time, a tall thin man with glasses and traces of his father in his face and stiff hair, his black eyebrows, the line of his jaw. His name is Chou Hai-en and he is now fifty-one years old. He said he remembered me from pictures he had seen and when he heard I was here wanted to come "to pay respects." He would have come sooner, he said, but returned only the day before from a trip to Canton. He is a technician on the staff of the national radio and TV network, he explained, but is currently on leave from that job to help in the arrangements for next year's 100th anniversary celebration of his father's birth. "I was his only son," he said, "It is a responsibility."

What has it meant to be Lu Hsun's son? "Advantages and disadvantages," he replied. "The people who hated my father also hated my mother and me. This was true from long ago right up until now. There are some people—it is inconvenient to mention their names—who still hate us. There is a Chinese proverb: if you want to make a person uncomfortable, give him small shoes to wear. Some people still try to make me fit into small shoes." But is it not also hard to fit into larger shoes? "Yes," he answered without change of expression, "that is also a disadvantage."

How had he made out during the Cultural Revolution? "I didn't suffer. They asked me questions. I was questioned a lot. But there was no result. I continued going to my job but for some months was given no work to do. After that I did some work. They did not dare to do anything to me openly because of my father."

And your mother? "My mother died in 1968. She died of great

anger. Chiang Ching sent people to our house who took away all Lu Hsun's letters. My mother was furious. She wrote to the Central Committee demanding that they be returned. She kept asking for them and they kept telling her that the letters could not be found. She suffered from heart trouble and on March 6, 1968, she died of heart failure. She was seventy years old. That night Chou En-lai came to the house and I gave him a letter my mother had written. He ordered an investigation. As a result the letters were found at the end of 1968 in Chiang Ching's house. They are now in the Lu Hsun Museum here in Beijing.''

Unfortunately Lu Hsun's son made this visit a "brief call" and very little time had been left for it. Our small fragment of talk was broken off. We shook hands and he left.

CHEN HAN-SENG

Of all our friends in Shanghai in those days, Chen Han-seng was probably the one we knew best, together with his wife Shu-shing. Han-seng was then already a noted agrarian economist, member of the Academia Sinica, author of a book on China's rural problems. He was also a salty-minded and salty-tongued man, fifteen years older than we were—in 1932 that made him thirty-seven to our twenty-two—slight, slender, dark, intense, his high-pitched voice breaking as he raised it, as he often did, whether in anger or sarcasm, irony, humor, with a half-lisp that sometimes seemed to trip his fluent English. He was a Kiangsu man himself, I think, and I remember him when he came back from his first trip to Canton, marveling about the Cantonese, speaking of them as if he had just been to another country, continent, even planet, astonished at their vigor and energy. The mercurial and all-knowing Han-seng was a regular contributor to the *China Forum,* author of a column on Chinese politics signed "Observer," reporting in vivid detail all the current intrigues and inner goings and comings in Kuomintang factional affairs. He used to dictate it to me and it would appear with only minor smoothing, paring, editing, one of the most avidly read features of the *Forum,* I am sure, not only by Chinese but by foreign readers who did not find that kind of information about Chinese politics anywhere else.

My parting from the Communists and the end of the *Forum* in 1934 was also a parting from Han-seng. I saw him next in 1944 in New Delhi where he was working for the British Ministry of Information, doing propaganda broadcasts in Chinese. We saw him again in New York in 1948 where he worked for a time at the Institute of Pacific Relations, a research group heavily influenced for some years by Communist-oriented members of its staff. The civil war was on in China. In the United States the debate was going on over the issue of American aid to Chiang Kai-shek and the hopeless effort to "save China" from the Communist onslaught. I last saw Han-seng one day late that year when he came to see me at my *Newsweek* office. We talked about the civil war. I often used to say in those days that if I were a Chinese, I would be shooting at the Kuomintang and getting shot from behind by the Communists. Whether it was this or some other remark critical of the Communists I do not recall, but something I said touched off a stormy attack in which he loaded on to me the rage he felt at the American aid being given to Chiang Kai-shek in the civil war. "My house is on fire," he all but screamed at me, "and you are pouring on the fuel, you are destroying us!" He made me the villain of the piece and I could only stand there, appalled, aghast, silenced, until he stopped shouting at me and left.

The wounds of that day bled somewhere in me through all the years from then until we met again on the evening of our arrival in Peking at the welcoming dinner given for us by the Writers Association. Han-seng, the old friend I never expected to see, was there. He embraced us in warm greeting, still a slight man, now eighty-five years old, his head, with its stubble of gray hair, thrown back so that he could peer at us through half-closed cataract-covered eyes, his voice high-pitched, insistent, as it always was. He gave no sign that he remembered anything about our last meeting, and why, I thought, should he, wondering now a little ruefully why I for my part had never forgotten it.

During that dinner, we fixed a time for a morning's talk. His place, which our driver had some trouble finding, was down a narrow alley between two shops opening into a wide and cluttered space where the old grid of houses and courtyards had been bulldozed away and a new building was going up, one of those squat plain five or six story structures that now cover so much of the ground back of the main avenues in downtown Peking. We had to pick our way through the debris and piles of material to the corner of the last of the old housing that still stood there. A few feet in from its torn and jagged edge, looking as if it had been left that way by a bomb or shell, Han-seng stood in an open doorway, greeting us as we came to it: "Welcome to World War Three!" he exclaimed in that piping, always-sardonic voice. He ushered us in-

With Han-seng and Shu-shing, Shanghai, 1933

to his surviving rooms, a workroom with a cluttered desk, a picture of Shu-shing on the wall. We asked about Shu-shing and he told us she had died.

She died one day in 1968 while he was a prisoner of the Cultural Revolution. He was confined to a room in the Research Institute for the Study of International Affairs in the Foreign Ministry. He stayed in that room for fourteen months. "I was not allowed to see anybody," he said, "so I never saw Shu-shing, who I knew was sick with cancer. I never had any news of her. Then they came in on the morning of November 6 and told me that my wife had died the day before, on November 5. Three people were sent with me here to this house. They were Party members on the staff of the Institute, one woman and two men, all in their forties. Her body was still in the courtyard. I went inside to her room and saw this man there, I knew him, he had once been a chauffeur in the East German embassy. He was there in that room. He picked up Shu-shing's wristwatch, a hexagon-shaped gold watch that had been given to her by some friends in England. I said I wanted to keep the watch as a memento. He said: 'Mind your own business. You are not qualified to talk!' He put the watch in his pocket as we left the room. I asked to go with the body to the east suburb for cremation but was told no, I could not be allowed to go. So I stayed there in the house for a while. I found some paper money that I gave to two women who had helped Shu-shing. Then I was taken back to my room of confinement at the Institute."

Like others of his generation in the Party, Han-seng was accused of crimes of betrayal decades before. "I was interrogated about a man who had been my assistant at the Academia Sinica way back in the 1930s. I learned that he had written a memorandum describing me as an agent of the CC clique in the Shanghai days." The "CC clique" was a group of top Kuomintang officials and politicians close to Chiang Kai-shek. It was headed by Chen Li-fu and his brother, Chen Kuo-fu. Among other things, they were in charge of the regime's anti-Communist ideological and propaganda activities as well as the extra-legal secret police and goon squads. "That fellow who wrote the accusation against me based it on the fact that one day Chen Li-fu asked Tsai Yuan-pei [director of the Academia Sinica] to send me to the Central Propaganda Headquarters to give a lecture, which I did. The subject was 'Taxes and Rent.' That fellow, who turned this into an accusation against me, is still right here in Beijing now, in a high office too. They kept coming to interrogate me, one of them a military officer. They would ridicule me, call me a fool."

It took six years for Chen Han-seng to clear himself of this charge. This was finally accomplished, he explained, when investigators went to some "real CC clique people" to get their testimony on the matter. That there were some "real CC clique people" in Peking to ask is a fact that illuminates some of the ways of political life in Communist China. In 1949, Hen-seng went on, when the Communist army was approaching Nanking, a group of the CC clique politicians negotiated a deal for handing over the city without further fighting. Part of the deal was assurance of their own future safety in the new regime. The compact was kept. All of them were living out their lives "in safe places" in Peking untouched by the storms of anti-rightist campaigns or cultural revolutions. When they were asked, they told investigators that Chen Han-seng had never been an agent of their group. Only then was the charge dropped.

"There was another case made against me," Han-seng went on. "I organized the magazine *China Reconstructs* [he was associated in this enterprise with Soong Ching-ling] and I recruited a Chinese-American woman to help me with it. They came to me while I was in confinement and asked me to write a statement saying she was an American agent. I said no, she was nothing of the kind. The next morning they came again and asked me if I had written what they had asked for, I said no, I couldn't do that, the charge was false. Then this fellow, about thirty, began to beat me. I shouted for help. Other people came running and stopped him." Han-seng was seventy-two years old at the time of that incident. It is one of the facts of post-Gang of Four life in Peking that the young man who began to beat him that day is still on the staff of that institute, still works at his job down the hall.

Han-seng remained in confinement for fourteen months. He was allowed no visitors, no reading matter. After his release, he lived for all the remaining years of the Cultural Revolution in a fragile freedom maintained by his silence. His release came about through the operation of that familiar controlling factor in Chinese Communist political life, *kuanshi,* the influence of personal connections. Han-seng profited at this critical juncture because of a link early in his Party life to a Party functionary named Kang Sheng. It was another glimpse inside this Communist miasma. Telling me about it, Han-seng told me more of his history than I had ever known in the early days. At that time, indeed, I was left to assume that he was a "sympathizer" like myself, functioning out in public rather than inside as a Party member; it was something about which one did not ask. Now I learned that not only was he a Party member but he was functioning in Shanghai as part of the Comintern apparatus, one of the small number of individuals, some of them Europeans, who led "public" lives in the city while carrying out their political activities undercover. Han-seng had become part of the Comintern staff as far back as 1925. In 1927, when the revolution was crushed in China, he fled to Moscow. He entered upon a career as a Comintern agent that took him to Japan and Europe, back to Shanghai during the years I knew him, and back to Moscow again. In Moscow in 1935, he was transferred from the Comintern apparatus back to the Chinese Communist Party. The Party official who arranged this transfer was his old friend Kang Sheng. Indeed, Kang Sheng's wife came to work for Han-seng in his new Party assignment.

Now it happened that by the time of the onset of the Cultural Revolution in 1966, Kang Sheng had risen to become one of Mao Tse-tung's close aides as a top hatchet man and high official in the secret police. In this role he was at the right hand of Mao's wife, Chiang Ching, in conducting the purges and punishments being meted out on all sides. In the Chinese way of things, this meant that charges against Chen Han-seng as an enemy of the Party would throw the blight of responsibility on his Party sponsor. This is why the charges laid against Han-seng were pushed back to a time before his connection with Kang Sheng. The connection was enough to save Han-seng from the much worse fates meted out to others of his years, especially since it had proved difficult to make the charges stick. All that Han-seng had to do to weather the cultural revolutionary storm for the rest of the time was to wait it out in silence, an ordeal that must have been almost as painful for him as imprisonment.

Han-seng supplied a second reason for his survival. He had avoided taking on any important job. "In January 1951," he said, "Chou En-lai asked me to be Deputy Minister of Foreign Affairs. I declined, because I am not an administrator, only a bookworm who can do research. Then they asked me to become vice-chancellor of Peida [Peking National University] where I once taught long ago. I said no, because Peida had been made into a copy of a Russian university, no general courses, no literature, no psychology, or history. Instead they had 'mind and matter,' dynastic studies, narrow topics, instead of the Anglo-Saxon style of general education followed by specialized work. I did do some lecturing at Peida at that time, and also at the new People's University. I found that no one laughed at my jokes, no one even smiled. Nobody asked questions. I asked why this was so and they told me that the Russian specialists teaching there at that time objected to smiles, they thought they were being laughed at, ridiculed. So they ordered their students to write out any questions they had for their Russian professors and hand them into the office, so it could first be seen if they were good questions, in which case they were handed on to the professors, who then sent their answers back written in Russian. It took a week to get an answer to a student's question! In those days when a Russian farted, some people here said, 'How fragrant!'"

But it was not just the Russian style, it was the Russian experience, he said, that led him to refuse the big jobs he was offered. "I refused posts because I foresaw trouble. People in such posts are the most likely to be sacked, and worse. In Russia when I was there in 1935-36, many of my friends were killed or killed themselves. The same thing happened here in the Cultural Revolution up to just a year or so ago. I expected this. I expected the same thing as the Russian purges here. And it *was* disastrous here, some twenty million people were affected, so many died, so many were persecuted, so many committed suicide. I don't think it will happen again, not again to such an extent. But I am a student of history. I allow for all that. I go on doing what I can."

And what is that, I asked this man of eighty-five who could hardly see. "What I am doing is helping young people to read, write, do work. I am trying to get young people into the Academy of Sciences. I am helping graduate students write their theses. I am editing an encyclopedia of foreign history to help educate the young ones who want to study. The future depends on them, on our helping the diligent." The new government was taking the right direction, he said, "but there are tremendous difficulties, tremendous difficulties."

He went on to talk about Mao Tse-tung, about current affairs—I will bring his observations on these matters together with others later on in these notes—but it was now past noontime. His niece came in with a whispered message. It was time for us to go. At the door that opened on to the bulldozed mess outside, Han-seng grasped my hand. He said: "You know, we come from different places, we've had different lives, but we have the same kind of mind." He raised his head to peer at me through his cataracts. All I could say was goodbye and good luck. Viola and he exchanged a hug. He stood in the doorway until we had picked our way across the cluttered ground to the waiting car. We left him there, waving his arm, like a survivor of an earthquake standing amid its ruins. And so he was.

THE DOCTORED PHOTO

I mentioned earlier that Tang Tao, one of the writers who came to see us about items in Lu Hsun's diary, presented us with a book of his newly published essays open to a page with a photograph which he eagerly pointed out to me because I was in it. It was a picture of a group taken in the garden of Soong Ching-ling's house on a day in 1933 when George Bernard Shaw came to lunch. In the group, left to right, were Agnes Smedley, Shaw, Soong Ching-ling, myself, dark hair glinting in the sunlight, most of me covered by the figure of Tsai Yuan-pei, the liberal educator. Next to him was Lin Yu-tang, at that time one of the editors of a Shanghai journal, *China Critic,* in which he wrote a column already well-known for its sardonic humor. Finally, at the far right, stood the small figure of Lu Hsun, with his stiff black hair, his brush of a mustache and heavy dark brows, squinting at the camera. I stared at the picture with a sudden rush of memory and feeling. I remembered the occasion well, if not this picture, and I was glad to have it as a souvenir. Just how much of a souvenir it was, I had yet to learn.

A few days later, when we left Peking for Shanghai, another double exposure took me back again nearly fifty years. As we taxied for takeoff in the Chinese airline's Boeing 707, I saw a pair of oxen pulling a plow in a field alongside the runway. It brought instantly to mind a sight like this that I put into the first sentence I wrote—in our house in Peking on a summer day in 1934—to open *The Tragedy of the Chinese Revolution:* "On the fringes of Chinese cities, the shadows of lofty chimneys fall across fields still tilled with wooden plows." That sentence came directly from a scene that lay before Viola and me one day as we walked on the outskirts of Shanghai. The lofty chimney belonged to the

The lunch party at Soong Ching-ling's, Shanghai, 1933, before and after doctoring

Shanghai Power Company plant, the wooden plow to the farmer tilling his small plot of ground at the very edge of China's greatest metropolis. This time I could not see what kind of plow those oxen were pulling as we roared past, the shadow of our great jet airplane falling upon them as we went by, a scene recording the persistence of China's crippling contrasts through this half century of our years.

As we pulled up into the gray sky, I was scribbling a note about this swift vignette. Viola pulled out of her bag a copy of the journal *Chinese Literature* given to us the day before by a woman writer, Shen Jong, because it contained an English translation of a long story she had written. While I wrote away in my notebook, Viola read her story, then began thumbing through the rest of the magazine. She stopped suddenly at a page she came to, sat up, thrust it at me. It was the beginning of an article about Agnes Smedley by two American admirers. Covering half the page was a photograph, the same picture of that group in Soong Ching-ling's garden, but not quite the same. Where I stood in the photo we had seen in Tang Tao's book, next to Soong Ching-ling and behind Tsai Yuan-pei, there was nothing but the dark shadow of the verandah. Next to Tsai Yuan-pei stood, not Lin Yu-tang, who had similarly disappeared, but Lu Hsun, whose small figure had been moved over to fill the space where Lin's had been. The two of us had vanished, brushed away into the limbo of non-personhood as totally as if the brusher had been an executioner seeing to it that we existed no longer, certainly no longer in that garden on that day nearly fifty years ago.

I stared at the picture, its impact coming hard and slow. So much had already made this a journey in a time capsule, a return to China across a gap a lifetime wide. My return from the outer world was hardly like but not wholly unlike the return of the old friends I was re-encountering just back from *their* limbos, in prisons, on labor farms, in distant places of exile, in confinement, in isolation. The welcome they gave us felt uncomfortably at times like the rehabilitation they had just experienced, old "errors" expunged, old labels removed, books put back on shelves, names restored, existence regained after all their years as non-persons. I had been feeling at secondhand all week the sensations of their non-personhood. Now with a force no mere empathy could match, I could feel these sensations as my own. I had just reappeared out of the shadow of Soong Ching-ling's verandah, just as they had reappeared out of the bournes from which they and so many others had just returned. In this picture before me, my twenty-three-year-old figure had disappeared, along with my youth, and here I was, seventy now, staring at the empty space, knowing acutely that for all who ever knew me then, including some of the friends I was re-encountering, I had simply not existed at all in the many years from that time until my return, that the person who appeared to them now, an aging man with a lifetime of other experience and work of which they knew nothing, was still only that dark-haired young man who had shared a little in the challenges and terrors they had faced in those days.

After a long minute, Viola and I began to talk about how we could get another copy of Tang Tao's book in which we had seen the original of this photograph—we had already mailed his book home along with others we had received—thinking that some Shanghai bookstore might have it and thus give us the means to take the matter up with our Writers Association hosts, and with the editor of this journal, none other than Mao Tun himself. But the ordained quality of so much that was present in this journey took care of this problem too. The next morning in Shanghai, our first call was at the Lu Hsun Museum where, as visitors who had been friends of the great man himself, we were received as very important guests. The entire staff was waiting at the entrance to greet us and the director, Mrs. Yang Lee, came forward holding out to us in her hand, as a welcoming gift, a glossy print of this same photograph in its original version, my certificate not just of rehabilitation but of veritable resurrection.

In the museum, the memorabilia of Lu Hsun's life were arranged in a series of exhibits showing the context of turbulent historic events of his years, from the last decades of the Manchu Dynasty, which fell in 1911, to the onset of Japan's war on China in the 1930s. The exhibits were arranged by the years of his life and the activities that filled them. Among those that covered the early 1930s, a number had to do with the China League for Civil Rights of which I have already written in these notes. Lu Hsun joined Soong Ching-ling in that bold attempt to challenge Chiang Kai-shek's regime of terror against opponents. Lin Yu-tang was one of the small number of Chinese liberals drawn to join them in this effort, attracted by their boldness, the protective cover of their prestige, and the small additional measure of protection afforded by foreign power in the International Settlement of Shanghai. When Yang Chien, a leading figure in the League, was murdered by Kuomintang assassins on a Settlement street one day in June 1933, many of these individuals, including Lin Yu-tang, shrank away, understandably afraid of the consequences of daring to persist. Newspaper clippings and magazine articles about all of this covered a section of a wall in the Lu Hsun Museum. Since I had had some part in this activity, my name appeared among the others in more than a few places. And there, in one of the large glass-covered panels of this exhibit, was the same photo of the group in Soong Ching-ling's garden, in its original undoctored form. That group gathered for lunch with Shaw that day was in fact the executive committee of the League for Civil Rights. We hoped, vainly as it turned out, that we could get Shaw to denounce Kuomintang repression and make a worldwide propaganda score with whatever he might say about it. Unfortunately, and to our considerable chagrin, we found we never could keep the aging Shaw's attention focused long enough on the matters that interested us. But there was the picture to mark the occasion, up on this wall not because of Shaw but because Lu Hsun was in it. As I stepped up to look more closely, I could see, however, that the Chinese caption under it was less than complete. There was a small stir of embarrassment among my hosts when I asked for it to be read out: "Smedley, Shaw, Soong Ching-ling, Tsai Yuan-pei, Lu Hsun, *and others.*" My writ of rehabilitation apparently restored my face but not my name. "I see," I said, and we went on with our tour of the museum.

Outside later, when we were leaving, a photographer was waiting to memorialize our visit. He took a picture of us standing in the middle of the group of museum staff and Writers Association hosts. After it was taken, I rather formally told Mrs. Yang that I would be most pleased if I could have a copy of it and would she please write on the back of it the names of all those present. "*All* the names," I said, "with no 'and others'!" At which the entire group broke into a relieved and relieving guffaw of appreciative laughter.

It was not easy in the circumstances to pursue the matter of the doctored photo. We were guests, our hosts were treating us with the full measure of Chinese courtesy, and we were Chinese enough ourselves in this respect to be unable to press them with embarrassing questions. From Shanghai, I wrote Mao Tun in Peking, since as honorary chairman of the Writers Association he was formally our host-in-chief, as well as nominal editor of the journal in which the doctored picture appeared. I made inquiry about it, I wrote, in the spirit of Teng Hsiao-ping's injunction "to seek truth from facts," expressing the hope that the current effort of the new leadership in China to turn away from the practices of the past would include those that involved the real or symbolic destruction of persons who for one reason or another did not please those in power.

At a dinner we gave before leaving Shanghai to thank our hosts for their hospitality, I raised the matter of the doctoring of photos and texts, a familiar practice of Communist demonology in Russia where millions of bodies lie in gulag graves but where also great masses of printed material, photographs, encyclopedia entries, histories, historic documents, and who knows what more, lie shredded or dissolved somewhere in the vast bottomlessness of the KGB's memory chutes. In China too, my guests assured me, and they recited examples, all drawn, to be sure, only from the recent era of the villainous Gang of Four. The most notorious and most hilariously recounted was a photo that showed Teng Hsiao-ping standing next to Mao Tse-tung on the wall at Tienanmen. The Gang-of-Four photo doctors had simply severed Teng's head and placed another head on his short and stocky body. More current examples were cruder still, the brush being used not to deceive but simply to exorcise the evil ones. Pictures that showed Mao's widow Chiang Ching and members of her Gang in places of power around Mao had been altered simply by removing their figures, leaving the empty places to show where they had stood once but would never, they all hoped, stand again.

Common as the practice apparently was, I continued to find it difficult to imagine why any Chinese would have felt reason enough to brush those two figures, of myself and Lin Yu-tang, from this particular picture. It is true that we both, in our very different ways, had become "counter-revolutionary enemies of the people." I had done so by splitting from my Communist friends in 1934 as a dissident on the left. Lin moved in the opposite direction, eventually all the way to becoming an ardent anti-Communist supporter of Chiang Kai-shek's Kuomintang. Still, it seemed to me that doctoring of this kind, whether in Russia or in China, would have to be applied to figures of some importance, whether factionally or otherwise. In this case, someone had been moved to blot out two individuals who had no such importance at all. I could easily have been relegated for all posterity to the category of "unidentified man"—as the caption at the museum did by merely omitting my name—and Lin too, who despite his later vogue among some Western readers for some of his books about China could have been depended upon to slide off into obscurity. He had already done so when I saw him five years ago in Hong Kong, failing from a stroke and soon to die. He was living the lonely life of an all-but-forgotten man who had himself forgotten most of what had passed earlier in his life, a pathetic mutual erasure. No, I felt a chillingly personal touch in the symbolic murders that had removed us from this picture. I could only wonder for whom this might have been important, important enough to go to the trouble of leaving only Agnes Smedley visible in that otherwise distinguished company.

However all that might be, the symbolic murder does seem to have been undone. I do not know who took me out of the picture, why, when, or where. Somebody—I do not know who, why, or how—dug up my airbrushed body and put me back into the picture. At our farewell dinner, Mrs. Yang announced, amid general nodding approval around the table, that she was going to restore my name to the caption in her exhibit. Her promise kept, I would not only be back from non-existence but—at least on the wall of the Lu Hsun Museum in Shanghai—also saved from namelessness. I obviously had to be as grateful as possible for this small favor.

* * *

Mao Tun's answer to our letter arrived a few weeks after our return home. The journal, he said, had obtained the doctored photo from the files of the Hsin Hua News Agency which had taken it from an album about Lu Hsun published in 1976, a time, he went on, "when many abnormal practices prevailed," a reference to the Gang of Four and the Cultural Revolution. He had advised the news agency, he said, "to take measures against the recurrence of such incidents."

Other inquiries produced some bits of additional information.

In its doctored form, this photo has apparently been around for many years. A copy of it turned up as an illustration only a year or so ago in a new edition of an old book by John Fairbank. Inquiry to the publishers produced the information that it had been obtained from an agency in New York called Eastfoto, which appears to be an agency for Soviet photos. In China, I was informed, it hung for a long time among the exhibits at the Lu Hsun Museum in Peking, and possibly also in Shanghai. It was used as one of the packet of postcards sold as Lu Hsun mementoes in both places. I received a copy of that postcard, showing the picture with only five figures, but oddly, in the caption on its back, listing—like the caption I saw in Shanghai—the five names and adding "and others." By some action by someone, unknown to me, the original, with all seven figures in it, began to reappear in 1979, turning up not only at the Lu Hsun Museum but also in a number of newly published books, like Tang Tao's essays and a new biography of Tsai Yuan-pei. I have tried in letters to learn more of how this came about, but all my inquiries have been turned away with polite non-replies. I reappeared by name as well as by face when this photograph in its original undoctored form appeared among many others in connection with special articles and supplements about Soong Ching-ling after her death in May 1981, as in *Beijing Review* (June 8, 1981) and *China Reconstructs* (September 1981), with full captions, and others, all including "American journalist Harold Isaacs" and "modern prose writer Lin Yu-tang." With Soong Ching-ling gone, I became the only one in that picture still alive, left alone to record the sensations of this experience of symbolic death and resurrection.

Shanghai, October 22

We walked along the Bund, still much as it was, except that its imposing row of pillar-fronted temples of trade and finance were grimier and blacker than they were and less imposing than I remembered them. Perhaps they looked larger in my mind's eye because of the power they used to house and smaller now because that power is gone. These ugly monuments to an ugly past of Western arrogance and cupidity are now occupied by Chinese successors in *their* banks and trading companies. They are servants of the State under the new dispensation, but it is difficult to imagine that all or even many of those who now sit in these seats of the mighty are models of selfless devotion to some larger public weal. The gap between those at the top of these institutions and the masses in the streets yawns only a trifle more narrowly than it did in the past.

In those streets now there were no man-pulled rickshas, though some man-pulled carts still carried heavy loads through the traffic. Cars and trucks were far more numerous here than in Peking, but not as thick as the crowds that jammed the sidewalks and the narrow strip of park bordering the Whangpoo. Most of these people looked better dressed and better off than Shanghai street crowds used to look, and they were not scurrying anywhere on any urgent business, just strolling as on a holiday afternoon. We had to search for an opening where we could lean for a moment on the heavy stone wall edging the walk to look out at the busy river. There were no foreign warships flaunting their mastery but the port scene was otherwise familiar, freighters, tugs, sampans, and what looked like a much-enlarged stretch of wharves and factories along the opposite bank in Pootung.

But our inner eye view carried little in it of any of these large features, past or present. It was focused instead on the figures of the two of us on that hot late August afternoon in 1932, Viola at the rail of a tender coming alongside the jetty—we found a recognizable piece of it still there in the changed clutter of wharf and landing platforms and moving people and carts of goods—and I on the jetty itself, each of us scanning the confusion with eager eyes to glimpse the other. Her ship, the *Empress of Asia,* had been three weeks bringing her across the Pacific and had been held up all morning in the river mouth because of a missed tide. She had waited with worried impatience; a wire she had sent me the night before had been reported back undeliverable. Those were the weeks when I had been under heavy pressure from both Kuomintang and American authorities, and she had no idea of what the situation might be when she arrived. The undelivered telegram was not a reassuring sign. But it was undelivered only because I had moved from the boarding house where I lived to the apartment I had taken for us in the spanking new Embankment Building, only a dozen or so blocks from where I stood waiting for her. I left the apartment at dawn that morning to wander up and down the Bund waiting for her to arrive, waiting for the coming of the new tide in my own affairs, much deeper, stronger, more lasting than the river's which did finally turn after midday and bring her to that jetty's side to that moment of reunion that became the beginning of all the rest of our lives. I arranged to have her baggage delivered and we set off to walk this same stretch of the Bund to its end, then to Szechuen Road (as Shanghai spelled it then, it was later rendered as Szechwan, now as Sichuan), across the bridge over Soochow Creek, left at the post office and on up the street to the Embankment Building.

We took that walk again this afternoon, more than forty-eight years later, hand in hand through the crowds and the traffic, around past Yuen Ming Yuen Road where I had my first *China Forum* office until my horrified missionary landlords evicted me, and where Viola taught at the Shanghai University night school, and halfway across the Szechuen Road Bridge where we stopped to take in the scene, so much the same, so different. Missing was the jam of small sampans moving on the creek or tied up along its banks, women cooking, children clambering, family wash fluttering on poles like streamers of signal flags identifying these small craft as the homes of those who plied their creek and river trade. Instead there were now mostly big motor barges, some tied in tandem tow, making their swift way through the blackened water, churning up heavy wakes that splashed high against the built-up banks. And over there was the Embankment Building, a great black hulk. From where we stood on the bridge, we could pick out the approximate location of that second-floor balcony from which we used to see and hear the vivid sounds of the life passing us in restless flow below. Because Lu Hsun had come to dinner with us there, the collectors at the Lu Hsun Museum had a picture they showed us of the building as it looked when, like us, it was young and new. It was so new when we moved in that it was still getting its finishing touches. A few mornings after our arrival, a workman in a bos'n's chair swung right into our open bedroom window for a moment of hilarious confusion as we confronted each other, we from under our hastily pulled-up covers, he halfway through the window, grinning at us.

We lived a busy life in that building for a year and a half, Viola off to her teaching job mornings at the Ta Tsun Middle School, some evenings at the university night school; I out to my continuing adventures with the *China Forum,* though much work was

Shanghai, 1932

done in the apartment itself. For several lengthy spells, especially after we started publishing in Chinese as well as English, one of our translators moved in with us, sleeping on our living room couch, safer there out of sight than he would have been coming and going to the *Forum* shop every day. Our table was a busy one, frequent lunches and dinners served to guests in haute cuisine Chinese or European style by our cook Ching, old enough to father us with smiling tolerance of our youth and our odd ways. He never inquired about our sleep-in assistants, no doubt assuming that like so many foreigners in Shanghai we were up to no good and that whatever it was, the less he knew about it the better. I cannot imagine that he was not approached to spy on us, but my guess is that he was able to display such impenetrable ignorance about our doings as to cause any police questioners to give up trying.

We went out to dinner frequently at Chinese restaurants—Shanghai's best were superb and not at all swanky—and often as guests of Chinese friends who did not entertain in their modest homes. We lived quite outside the foreign community's club life and the city's notorious night life and we never missed either. We had our fun, a lot of it, in our own small circle, took in American and European movies as they came along, went occasionally with friends to Chinese opera, almost always enjoying more of what went on in the audience than on the stage. We went on picnic excursions around Shanghai's outskirts and a few times farther out by train to Soochow where we were poled in a gondola-like sampan through its Venice-like canals, something we did one day under an unrelentingly steady rain. Another time we went for an unforgettable weekend by small steamer down the coast to the temple island of Pootoo, off the coast of Chekiang, walking for most of a long day, stopping to plunge into the sea or lie on the warm sand along its miles of blessedly deserted beaches. We did not want for sweet respites, whether in company or the two of us by ourselves, from the bitter tea of the larger day-to-day events that were the main business of our working and thinking lives.

All this and more unrolled like a reel of film before us as we leaned on the parapet of the Szechuen Road Bridge and looked across at the apartment house where so much of it took place. We went no nearer. It is occupied now by deserving officials and Party cadres, we had been told, but we were content not to see it closer up in its present incarnation but rather to let our memories run as we looked at it, the traffic rolling past on the bridge behind us, the barges churning down the creek, the afternoon sky casting a bleak gray light over it all. After some minutes of silence, we turned to walk back into the crowded narrowness of Szechuen Road.

Much about our life in Shanghai happened on this and neighboring streets. I could identify the four-story building, unprepossessing then, more so now, where the *China Forum* had its office. Somewhere along here on the top floor of a similar building was the boarding house where I lived before Viola came. Up another street was the building where the *China Press* was located, and the American Club, which I had never entered. We went past the old Chinese YMCA where Nguyen Ai Quoc, later Ho Chi Minh, lived during those months of hiding. We stood across from the red stone and brick building that had housed the U.S. Consulate General, almost surely identifying it, we thought, by the large oval mark that could still be seen over its entrance where the consular shield had hung. This was where I had those encounters with the Consul General and the U.S. Attorney, and here was where we went a few days after Viola's arrival to register to be married. This caused a loud buzz in interested foreign dovecotes where the young vice consul with whom we recorded our honorable intentions (George V. Allen, whom I met often in later years as ambassador to India and Assistant Secretary of State) passed the word: "He's twenty-two, and she's twenty-two, and verrree nice!" When we went back ten days later to be married, we were quite unaware that when we were ushered into the office of a lower-ranking official for the brief ceremony, it was because the judge of the United States Court for China had refused to have anything to do with this obnoxious young Bolshevik.* The ceremony took only a few minutes. Viola had come from her class, I from my office, Frank Glass had come to stand as witness, needlessly, we discovered when we were all assembled. Afterward

---

*It was U.S. Commissioner Jacob Krisel, whose post was equivalent to that of magistrate in the extraterritorial American Court for China, who officiated. By odd chance some years later he met my father whose name reminded him of the incident. My father quoted him as saying that it would have been his duty in any case to act in Judge Purdy's place, but particularly so in this instance of a Jewish boy who was doing so many wrong things and wanted to do this one right thing by this nice girl.

we went our separate ways for the rest of the day. There has been nothing as brief or casual ever since about the way the bond formally sealed that day has lasted.

We turned at the intersection of Szechuen and Nanking Roads, busy in our time, busier now, and walked on toward the river, stopping to look into the lobbies of the two old hotels that still stood opposite each other where Nanking Road ended at the Bund. The old Palace and the old Cathay looked unchanged, only fifty years more wear showing, and they were still, ironically, hotels reserved for foreigners only. They were not as slickly maintained as they used to be. Large stretches of lobby space had been filled with exhibits for foreign tourists and businessmen. Shops for foreigners only (called "Friendship Stores") sold arrays of mass-produced replicas of Chinese "antiques" and artifacts of various kinds, as well as textiles and clothing, all producing foreign exchange at high profit from foreign visitors now coming in ever-increasing numbers and paying exorbitantly for the privilege of doing so.

Outside, at the corner of the Bund, as appointed, our hosts were waiting, anxious about our wandering around so long by ourselves, apparently afraid we might get lost or run into something untoward, as one well might in an encounter with the past. But now they had us safely back in their Writers Association car and we were driven up Nanking Road, onto what used to be called Bubbling Well Road, past the old race course, now a market, and across Tibet Road toward what used to be the French Concession. One of the buildings we passed was the hotel in which the Five Writers and Nineteen Others were arrested that night in 1931. We passed through the large open plaza where what had been called the Great World Amusement Palace still occupies its prominent corner, still apparently a public center and place of amusement. Here in this wide space, intersection of broad avenues at the border of the onetime Settlement and French Concession, the streets would be filled any night with prostitutes, often children of not more than nine or ten, and their vigilant amahs soliciting for them, with beggars crying their pleas, rickshas being pulled by in a steady stream or clustered at the curbs seeking customers. There was none of this now, no prostitutes, no beggars, no rickshas, only the thick traffic and the packed moving masses of darkly clad people looking in general better off than people used to look here without yet looking well off. Flashes of more colorful dress turned up here and there in the crowd, reappearing here now in what used to be a city of high style. There were still patched rags to be seen, some on men still pulling or bearing heavy loads, but few compared to the past when wretchedness among great numbers all but dominated this busy city scene.

We were put up in what were formerly known as the Grosvenor Apartments, a luxury complex which housed upper crust foreigners in the old days, close to the similar Cathay Mansions, all of these buildings together now reorganized as the Ching Chiang Hotel, exclusively reserved for the use of foreign travelers. Our room and bath, part of what had been a large apartment, was palatial in a badly worn and gloomy way, including palatially sized roaches free to move in and out at will, as Chinese still were not, but where the role of the actors in this class drama (not counting the Communist roaches as necessarily any more numerous than the capitalist-imperialist roaches of our day) had undergone a distinct change. Foreigners full of imperialist pelf who once lorded it here over their Chinese servants were still the guests and the Chinese were still the servants, but it did not need much of a glimpse of the tourist circuit with its deflated returns at inflated prices to see who were the exploiters now.

October 23

We went again to 29 Rue Moliere, now Shantsan Road, to the Sun Yat-sen house where Soong Ching-ling lived, where I had gone so often on the business of the *Forum,* the China League for Civil Rights, for working lunches, meetings, and, often, for warm and gay and wondrously delicious dinners. The house was looted by Japanese soldiers when they occupied the city in 1937. It was vandalized again by Red Guard hoodlums when they were turned loose by Mao Tse-tung and Mrs. Mao in 1966. It has been restored as a Sun Yat-sen Museum, filled with pictures and memorabilia of the founder of the Kuomintang who lived here for periods of time early in the century. The walls were covered with photographs, including some of the youthful Soong Ching-ling. The photographer who was following us around took a picture of me looking up at one enlarged photo-portrait of her as she was when I first knew her, about forty then, at what must have been her most beautiful maturity.

The house was a different place, the rooms rearranged. The wall along the stairway going up to the main living room was bare. Here is where those four panels hung that evening when I paused on our way up to admire them, only to have them arrive at our apartment door the next morning. These were the panels Soong Ching-ling told us in Peking she was glad to have given to us, for they would otherwise have been destroyed or lost. After our tour of the house, we were led out into the garden and posed for a group picture with the Museum staff. It was only a day or two later, when a copy of this picture was presented to us before our departure that we noticed it had been taken on the same spot as that older group picture in Soong Ching-ling's garden from which I had been blotted out for so many years.

WANG HSIN-TI

One of the representatives of the Writers Association who welcomed us on our arrival in Shanghai was Wang Hsin-ti, a short owlish-looking man with wispy gray hair and heavy glasses. He was with us during much of our brief stay in the city and we quickly learned to value his help as a guide and interpreter in some of our conversations, for he proved to be a well-schooled and knowing man who caught many of the overtones and undertones of our questions and the answers we were getting. When he came back to our hotel with us from our visit to the Lu Hsun Museum, I asked him about himself. What emerged was the story of a different kind of survivor of the hazards of life in these years in China.

Wang Hsin-ti came of "bad" origins, an urban bourgeois family that had prospered in the bad old days of foreign and Kuomintang rule. His father had begun as a clerk in the British-run Kailan Mining Administration, had risen to become a factory manager, acquired stock in the company, and sold it at the right time. Wang Hsin-ti was graduated from Tsinghua University in 1935, so that he was a student in Peking at the time we lived there. Two years later, just before the Japanese invaded north China, he went abroad to the University of Edinburgh to study English and English literature. He was on his way home from Scotland in 1939 when the war in Europe began. He got to Hong Kong where he had to choose between going to Chungking, where Chiang Kai-shek's government had its new wartime capital, or to Shanghai, where Western interests were still precariously holding on under the eye of the occupying Japanese and their puppet government in Nanking. "My family persuaded me to come to Shanghai," he said, "I came, and I have been here ever since."

This meant that Wang Hsin-ti lived through the Japanese years in Shanghai which ended in 1945, the four-year interregnum under the restored Kuomintang government which ended in 1949, and for thirty-one years since then under Communist rule. Through all of this, he survived by being what he had never thought to be, a banker and a business manager.

Wang Hsin-ti had always wanted to be a writer, a poet. He had a book of poems published in Peking in 1935. On his return from Scotland, he planned to combine writing with a teaching career and with help from a relative he did get a job at a Shanghai university. "I actually gave lectures on Shakespeare!" he exclaimed. But this lasted only two years. When the Japanese took over the whole of Shanghai after Pearl Harbor, they closed the universities. Wang's uncle came to his aid again and got him a job as secretary to the manager of the Kincheng Bank. "When I came to the bank, I didn't even know how to use an abacus!" Wang said with a laugh. "But in five years' time I got to be assistant manager, then sub-manager." At the end of 1947, he accompanied the general manager of the bank to New York, where he trained for some months at the Irving Trust Co. before returning to Shanghai in mid-1948.

"From the time I came back from Edinburgh," Wang said, "I did no writing. I had no contact with any intellectuals. When the Japanese took over, my friends said if I stayed in Shanghai I would have to join the Japanese side. I said no, I wouldn't, I was just a businessman, and I stayed on. My job at the bank helped me. If the Japanese knew I was a writer, I would have had trouble. Instead, no attention was paid to me. Through some clerks in the bank I got in touch with the Communist Party underground. I never had cared for the Kuomintang, I never liked what they did to people. And by this time I had a family myself—I married in 1940 and I have three daughters and a son. After the Japanese surrender in 1945, some of my friends who were writers came back from Chungking to Shanghai. They formed a Writers Assocation and I became secretary and treasurer and helped them get financial support. I began writing poetry again myself. I read Auden, Spender, Eliot. I wrote on lyrical themes or ironic poems. In 1947, I published my second volume of poetry."

When the Communists took over in Shanghai in 1949, it was not his poetry but his business experience that he could put at their disposal. He helped organize and operate what became the National Foodstuffs Manufacturing Company, a food processing operation which served a large area with its output. At some point in the 1950s he applied for membership in the Communist Party but was rejected because of his "bad" origins and because he had money. "This was my family fortune," he explained, worth about yuan 100,000 (just over U.S. $70,000 at the official rate of exchange). "I said I would give the money to the Party and then would join. They said no, I couldn't give them the money until I was allowed to enter the Party." Wang would not agree to this. "You see," he explained, "if I entered the Party with my money, I would have been seen as bourgeois; while if I had already surrendered the money and had nothing when I joined, I would already have proved that I was non-bourgeois, see?" I was not sure I did see, but I let the question go. Wang simply continued thereafter to serve in his useful job, rising to become sub-manager.

His problem remained his "label" which was "bourgeois" mitigated only by the designation "government employee." (The "label," readers will recall, was the tag identifying every individual on his official personal record, with decisive effect on his status and all conditions of his life.) He was managing fairly well for himself and his wife, but the burden fell upon his children as they grew up, especially on his third daughter because she aspired to become a member of the Communist Party. As a middle school senior, she went on a pilgrimage to Chingkangshan, the mountain-top Mao shrine in Kiangsi, and became fired with ambition to follow the Maoist inspiration. When she finished school she went to Kiangsi as a farm laborer—one of the army of young people sent out to the countryside to work as peasants. She worked as a farm laborer in Kiangsi for ten years, from 1968 to 1978. She applied there for membership in the Party but was rejected because her father was "bourgeois." In accordance with Chairman Mao's injunction to have nothing to do with the "bourgeoisie," she cut off all relations with her family beyond a very occasional letter.

"She would take no money from us," Wang said. "She did take some when she first went out, but no more. She was exceptional in this. Most of the young people who went to the countryside got subsidies of some kind from home. They could not support themselves out there with their own labor. Many did no work at all, just lived on what they got from home. Those who did work got very low pay for it. Chairman Mao ordered the students to the countryside, but in practice it did not work out. There were no concrete measures by local governments to help. The young people could not work out the difficulties by themselves. Most of them have come back now, but some are still there. Some got married and can't come back. Some who got married got divorced and came back alone. The returned students are now a serious social problem in the cities. The government has tried to help them get jobs, but they don't know how to do anything. All they ever did in their lives was a little farm work and maybe not even that. All they can do here now is labor at a very low wage. Most get no jobs at all, only a place on some waiting list, which means they just loaf around doing nothing.''

But Wang's third daughter was different. "She had a very strong will," he said with pride. This made a difference in the way she spent her years in the countryside and in what happened when she came back. "Out there she remained cut off from us. She trained herself to adapt to her environment. She maintained herself by her own hard work. This was very rare. It was hard for her. She went through much spiritual suffering. She had gone quite voluntarily to Kiangsi but she had to recognize the great differences between the students and the peasants. Kiangsi is strong in local feeling, all places are. She was treated badly by the peasants and this cooled down her zeal. But she kept working at it because she was convinced it was the correct thing to do according to Chairman Mao.'' But the years brought second thoughts, including disenchantment with Chairman Mao following upon the storms of the Cultural Revolution and the fall of the Gang of Four. She began to think there had to be more for her to do than spend her years as a peasant in Kiangsi. "She began to feel she had learned a lot from the peasants but she also began to regret that she was forgetting everything she learned at middle school.'' She began to take steps to move in a new direction and this brought her back to the matter of her father's unfortunate "bourgeois" label. But in this too, the times had brought change for the better.

Not long after the Cultural Revolution began in 1966, Wang said, his money was taken away from him—my notes are not clear on where this money was being kept all this time—but he was given a receipt for it. He went on working undisturbed at his job for the rest of that stressful time, but after the fall of the Gang of Four in 1976, his case was taken up again by the Party in Shanghai. "They asked me if I wanted the money back or wanted to give it up. They suggested that I take it back. I said no, I would give it up forever. After full consideration, they decided to accept the money and cleared me to join the Party. But I said no, I would wait and see. That was two years ago. I am still outside the Party and they are still keeping the door open for me.'' But one thing did get settled, and this was the matter of his ''label.'' He was close to retirement from his job and what he wanted most, he told the Party people, was to have his label changed from ''bourgeois'' to ''writer.'' This was done. He was now officially labeled as a ''writer'' and described as a ''close follower of the Party.'' This solved his problem and it solved his daughter's too. She applied again for Party membership and was accepted. She came back from Kiangsi, spent a year studying for the university entrance examination, passed with top grades, and entered Normal University in Shanghai. She was now thirty-three years old. Wang's other two daughters had already become teachers and his son had a job.

"I feel very lucky," Wang ruminated. "If I had been a writer before, I would have suffered like all writers did. If I had entered the Party, I would have been kicked out and suffered much difficulty." As it was, he retired from his job in 1979, staying on only as a consultant. Meanwhile he had already re-connected with the Writers Association and resumed his own writing, a book of essays and more poetry. After his retirement, he entered upon his new life's work full time. "I have written more poetry and done more reading in the last two years than in the last thirty years altogether," he said happily. Now sixty-nine, he was at last doing what he wanted to do.

WU CHIANG

The welcoming group from the Writers Association that met us when we arrived at the Shanghai airport was headed by the local vice-chairman, Wu Chiang, who also hosted the dinner given to us in the evening. He was a squat stocky hard-looking man who wore a western-style cap flat on his head and his coat buttoned up to his chin, giving the same squat and stocky look to his heavily lined face. He was the very picture of a tough cadre's cadre who had been through a great deal, as indeed we learned he had, from the time he began his career as a tyro writer in Shanghai in 1932. He met me then, he smilingly volunteered, at a meeting at the YMCA where he was one of those who formed a writers' anti-Japanese organization. We fixed a time to meet again at our hotel so that I could hear more of his story.

Wu Chiang was born in 1911 so he was now not quite seventy years old. This was old enough for him to have had some directly personal part in nearly all the turbulent history of China in this century, a common experience for members of his generation. In Wu Chiang's case, it even included some repercussions of the revolution that brought down the Manchu dynasty the year he was born. In the small northern Kiangsu village where he lived, his father, a poor shopkeeper, was one of many men who continued for years afterward to wear their queues, or pigtails—badges of Manchu overlordship—and made their sons do so as well. One could say Wu Chiang's political life began when he and some similarly afflicted schoolmates, tired of being ridiculed by boys from more enlightened families, tried to cut their pigtails off and were severely punished by their fathers. He was fourteen in 1925 when propagandists not much older than he came north to spread the word of the British shooting of Chinese students in Shanghai that May 30. He was sixteen when some of Chiang Kai-shek's soldiers came through the village looking for its "red elements," of whom Wu Chiang was one. He was in prison for a month, escaped execution because he was so young, and was released when some relatives put up money to buy him out. He went to school, became a teacher, but a few years later, after the Japanese attack in 1932, he went to Shanghai where he began his career as a writer and a Communist.

This took him to Honan in central China where he became a member of a propaganda group that toured the villages doing anti-Japanese playlets, some of which he wrote. One of the members of that group was Li Shin, our Writers Association host, ten years younger than Wu Chiang. "He played the part of a Japanese soldier," grinned Wu Chiang, "I played an old peasant." At the end of 1936, the Communists and Chiang Kai-shek's Kuomintang joined in a fragile new "united front" to fight the Japanese and the next year the war of resistance to the Japanese began in earnest. In 1938, Wu Chiang and Li Shin went to Hankow and then to Anhwei to join the Communist New Fourth Army. Li Shin went from there to Yenan but Wu Chiang stayed with the New Fourth Army through all the years of the Japanese war and the civil war against the Kuomintang that followed, rising to become head of its propaganda department with the rank of general. He left the army in 1952, after fourteen years, returned to Shanghai, where he served in various Party posts and in the Writers Association.

The next five years were filled with vivid and livid struggle among cultural bureaucrats and writers, and I wondered what Wu Chiang's own role had been in the harsh give and take between the ins and the outs during that time. He said only that during the brief period of the Blooming of the Hundred Flowers (the months in 1957 when Mao Tse-tung opened the spigot and all writers and intellectuals were invited to speak and write their minds freely), he had written an article "which urged that we remove the wall that had grown up between the Party and the people." When the spigot was abruptly closed and the "Anti-Rightist Campaign" was launched against all who had spoken up and against writers and intellectuals in general, Wu Chiang was arrested in that great sweep and imprisoned for a year. But he was lucky, he went on, and for a characteristically Chinese reason. "I was accused of being a 'Rightist,' but I didn't get the label put on me. The reason was that before publishing my article, I sent it to the Propaganda Ministry in Shanghai for censorship and they approved it for publication. Because of this, they could not give me the 'Rightist' label without involving themselves. So I escaped the worst. This showed that I was rather cautious in my ways."

Earlier that same year, 1957, the government press had published Wu Chiang's novel *Red Sun,* based on his army experience. It appeared in English translation in 1961, and also in Japanese, in editions published by the Foreign Languages Press in Peking. It disappeared in all its editions, however, when the Cultural Revolution began in 1966. "They attacked the novel because they wanted to attack Marshal Chen Yi, my commander, and the book depicts his victories, and also because at one point it showed a brigade commander who got drunk. They said it was wrong to show black on the face of the Liberation Army." Like his published work, Wu Chiang also disappeared into the limbo of the Cultural Revolution. Both reappeared about ten years later. He brought with him to our hotel this afternoon a copy of the new edition of his novel issued in both Chinese and English in 1978.

"First I was kept prisoner in a small office room in the Writers Association Building," he said. "Then after two months I was moved to the prison at Tsaohoching, west of Shanghai, which was also a prison in the Kuomintang time. There I was kept in total isolation for the first two years. The only thing I was allowed to write were confessions of my crimes. I wrote several hundred thousand words during that time. They kept coming to demand that I confess more and more. I was beaten with broad leather straps with brass buckles. They kept telling me that I was a Kuomintang traitor. I refused to agree with this. They beat me more, on my head and around my ears. I had to kneel on the stone on my bare knees for half an hour at a time. But many prisoners suffered much more than I did. Many committed suicide. While I was at the Writers Association building, three secretaries jumped from the top of it and died. At the prison, those scum kept saying to me: you can jump in the river any time. But I wouldn't. I refused to commit suicide. I wouldn't do it."

"What did you think about what was happening?" I asked. "This was your Party, your revolution, what did you think?" Wu

Chiang looked straight at me and without hesitation replied: "The Communist Party is a party of many years, a long history, many old cadres and generals. I was sure that if they survived, the truth would come out."

As fortune had it, some of these "old cadres and generals" did survive, did regain power, and did bring Wu Chiang and all the other surviving victims back from limbo. I pressed Wu Chiang about the chance of the triumph of the "truth" that saved him and about his feelings while he was going through his ordeal. But he responded only with all the current formulas about the "mistakes" of Mao Tse-tung and the promise of the new course under Teng Hsiao-ping. Wu Chiang remained cautious in his ways.

CHEN YI

How did Communist survivors of these hard times in Communist China deal with becoming victims of their own illusions, losing their best years not to any outside foe but to comrades of their own Party acting in the name of their great leader, Mao Tse-tung himself? In the various answers I got to this question, I heard the mingled accents of the stoic, the philosopher, the cynic, or the cautious survivor, and—in varying intensities—the true believer. Of the latter, the most striking example was supplied by Chen Yi, poet, playwright, onetime head of the Cultural Department of the Liberation Army with the rank of general (not to be confused with the military leader Marshal Chen Yi). Back after twenty-one years in limbo, Chen Yi was now Vice Secretary of the Party Secretariat in Shanghai.

Chen Yi was not someone I knew in the early 1930s but someone who knew me or of me because he was a reader of the *China Forum*. When he heard I was in Shanghai, he asked to see me. He appeared at the appointed time, thin gray hair, large staring eyes, gold teeth gleaming in a ravaged face, sixty-eight, he said he was, but older looking than that, wearing a well-pressed brown coat with leather edgings and blue trousers. He came in, hand outstretched with a broad smile of greeting and plunged right into telling me how as a young Communist of twenty in Peking he read the *Forum,* "published in those most difficult years, the darkest age of the Chinese revolution." In May 1933, he was arrested and sent to prison in Nanking. He was released in 1936 and made his way to the northwest where he joined Mao's 8th Route Army and began his career as a cultural worker in the military establishment. He served through the Japanese war, the civil war, and on into the years following the Communist victory in 1949. Those were the good years, he said, much good literature written, many good films made. Those were also the years of the heavy struggles in the bureaucratic machinery that ruled all that was called "culture" in China, shaped with a heavy hand from the first years. Chen Yi was part of the system until March 1958 when the heavy hand landed on him. Along with many others guilty of being writers and intellectuals, he was denounced and expelled as a "Rightist" and sent off, like Ting Ling, to Heilungkiang in northern Manchuria. There he remained for twenty-one years, most of them spent in farm labor camps, three of them in prison. His wife, exiled with him, was also imprisoned with him. "When we were in prison together," said Chen Yi, "I wrote a poem: 'We two in our places/ twelve meters between us/ but one thousand mountains apart.'" They could not see each other, only once in a while "we could hear each other's voices." Their children suffered for their father's sins. "My eldest was labeled 'counter-revolutionary' and sent to the countryside for eight years. My youngest daughter was in Harbin with us and simply had to shift for herself when we were in prison."

"Yes, those were difficult days and years," Chen Yi said, "hard to bear. I knew revolution was difficult, incomparably difficult. I felt strong enough to face any difficulties. But I would lie awake in the night and ask myself: what crime did I commit to get such harsh punishment? It was hard to bear, hard. But still, I lived through it.

"You can well ask how I got through all this. I had three things: I had the will to live. I was determined that no matter how people maltreated me, I would not maltreat myself. And finally I knew that as long as the Chinese Communist Party persisted in seeking the real 100 percent Marxist Party line, there could always be hope."

"One hundred percent Marxist Party line?" I asked in wonder.

"Yes. I am a fifty-year Party member, well-educated by the Party. I have strong convictions. As long as the Party continued to seek the true 100 percent Marxist Party line, there could be hope. I believed this."

"But Chen Yi," I said almost pleadingly. "There are a thousand 100 percent Marxist Party lines! The people who did all this to you, expelled you, sent you to labor camps, put you in prison, persecuted your children—they were *all* following a '100 percent

Marxist Party line'! How can you say this?'' We were not alone. Local officials of the Writers Association were sitting by listening, one of them serving as interpreter. Chen Yi stared at me, his large eyes glassy, reflecting the gray light from the window. He leaned forward and said urgently: ''I see you don't believe . . .'' He held out his hand. ''I ask you, I ask you, *believe* me!'' I stared back at him and then I made a small speech of my own. ''You have all been through your experience here,'' I said, ''but this has not been your experience alone. Our whole generation everywhere went through it in different ways, dreaming the great socialist dream, then having it crushed, by Stalin and his murderous regime in Russia and now again here in China. We were left to find some better way to human betterment, something better than prisons and labor camps and killings and oppression worse than before, and we haven't been very successful.'' I had to struggle to keep my voice down, my feelings in check. This man before me and others I had met had gone through their hells, had their lives ruined, and insisted that they remained true believers in a ''100 percent Marxist Party line.'' It was preposterous and if it were so, crushing. If I were to take Chen Yi at his word, I would have to see him and his fellows as Christian martyrs, appealing to a non-believer waiting with them to go out to the lions. ''Your return to life was purely providential,'' I said. ''If the Gang of Four had moved faster and grabbed power in time, what then?'' ''Why then,'' came the reply, ''we wouldn't be sitting here talking!'' Everyone laughed. No one responded to what I had said.

When I asked Chen Yi how he had been extricated from his plight, he told a familiar story, again a matter of personal connections. He had been first labeled ''Rightist'' and then, when the Cultural Revolution began, he was charged with betraying the Party from the beginning, from the time he was arrested in 1933. He had no trial or hearing but was released from prison in 1976 when the Cultural Revolution came to an end and the uneasy interregnum in Peking began. Chen Yi remained ''under control'' in Harbin for two years longer. When Teng Hsiao-ping finally put down the Gang of Four and took power into his hands, one of his chief aides was a somewhat younger Party veteran, Hu Yao-pang, who became general secretary of the Party. Hu Yao-pang, it so happened, was an old comrade of Chen Yi. Papers on his case moved swiftly then and his release was signed by Teng Hsiao-ping himself. By October 1978, Chen Yi was fully rehabilitated, all charges erased, his Party membership restored, and his rank as general, together with all his old salary and perquisites.

"Yes," continued Chen Yi, "if the Gang of Four had been successful, all would have suffered, but that is all gone now." And he was sure, he said, it could not happen again. "Given our present leadership and line," he said firmly, "we believe there is little chance of any such thing being repeated. The Central Committee has had many conferences. There have been many documents. All are centered on this problem, all searching for the right conclusion. It is still to be made, still to come. We are now experimenting, trying to do our best. That's what we are doing, what we have to do, to educate the young to have faith in the Party. We are in charge of youth education. We have to teach our sons and daughters to learn Marxist teachings, to distinguish the bad from the good."

I asked Chen Yi if he was writing his story. He avoided a direct answer. He displayed the now-familiar caution. The lesson of all this was that you could never be sure how what you wrote today would look tomorrow, and who would be there to do the looking. I quoted to Chen Yi those lines written by William Morris more than a hundred years ago: "Men fight and lose the battle, and the thing they fought for comes about in spite of their defeat, and when it comes it turns out to be not what they meant, and other men have to fight for what they meant under another name." He responded with his glassy smile. "As a Party member for fifty years," he said, "despite everything, I believe the present line of the leadership of the Central Committee is right!" And then he left.

One of those who had been in the room through the long afternoon of these exchanges came over to me and said: "I see you were wondering about their despair. They *do* feel despair. But they cannot let it come out."

OF
THE
LARGER
POLITICS

The only views I can report of the larger current political scene in China at the time of this visit have to be those glimpsed, reflected, or refracted in the conversations I had with a small number of people in a very brief space of time. The focus of these conversations was narrowly individual, not broadly general. Yet the two dimensions were of course not separable, not for these individuals whose entire lives were governed by their political experience. Some of what emerged about this in our talks I have saved from my notes to put together here where they have seemed to me to be matters of more than transitory interest as well as parts of the immediate setting in which these individual dramas were being played out.

Everyone to whom we listened during those days of encounter and re-encounter assured us that the new Party leadership under Teng Hsiao-ping had brought new freedom, perhaps even some measure of democracy, to political life in China. These particular individuals could say this feelingly on their own account: the new leadership had literally brought them back to life, back from prison, labor camp, exile, or years of house arrest and silence, had restored their identities not only as persons but as members of the Party, and given them the chance to participate as aging survivors in the politics they had helped to create. Mao was gone and his villainous Gang of Four ousted and put away and a new course was being set toward less ideology, more pragmatism, and more rapid modernization. Each one had to settle somehow on his or her inner personal sense of the meaning of this experience, a difficult, delicate, and dangerous matter touching emotional depths they generally chose not to explore, as "Marxist-Leninists" out of ideology, as Chinese out of deeply embedded cultural conditioning. But as "Marxist-Leninists" and as Chinese, they were well-practiced at raising subjective difficulties to objective levels, in this case rather easily done, since the questions that made for inner crisis were closely related to the questions that dominated the political scene to which they had returned, all of them also difficult, delicate, and dangerous.

What to say now about Mao Tse-tung? How much was he still hero, how much villain? How far was he to be held responsible for the crimes and disasters that filled most of his years in power, and did this guilt outweigh the achievements and victories of his early years? How to explain what happened to Mao, to the Party, the Revolution, the country? How to insure it would not happen again? How to face the mountainous problems that were the legacy of the Mao era? And perhaps most crucially, in post-Mao and post-Gang-of-Four China, how much democracy, how much freedom was there to be, and for whom? Where were the limits *now?*

These questions came up in all our talks with those we met. They were difficult because they bore on the whole fabric of politics, policy, and power. They were delicate because no one could be sure how matters would come out, the fate of the regime was at stake. They were dangerous because it would not do at all to find yourself on the wrong side of things again, especially if you were seventy or eighty years old, tired and sick, and had been through travail enough for your time. Hence, whether out of conviction or prudence or some mix of the two, everyone, young or old, subscribed to the going "Party line" as they understood it. With only marginal variations, where it was explicit, they were explicit; where it was tentative, they were tentative. To be sure, this still left room for a good deal of what by Chinese Communist standards could be called free and salty speech, though not as free as it would have been a year or half a year earlier (and a good deal freer than it was a year later).

Our visit took place well past the peak of tolerated freedom of expression that followed the events of 1976-78, the death of Mao, the end of the Cultural Revolution, the downfall of the Gang of Four, and the establishment of the new leadership under Teng Hsiao-ping. The starting point of this process is generally identified with the massive demonstration that took place in Peking on April 5, 1976, when several hundred thousand people poured into vast Tienanmen Square in what became an unauthorized act of mourning for Chou En-lai, the remarkably supple leader who had held on precariously through Mao's time, protected many of his friends from attack, and had become, by the time of his death in January that year, a symbol of moderate resistance to the extremism of the Mao regime. Teng Hsiao-ping, then back in the government during one of the several shifts at the top during this period, was accused of instigating the demonstration, was dismissed from his post and sent back into exile. Mao died in September 1976, his wife and her "Gang of Four" were arrested and Teng and his associates positioned themselves to take over the leadership of the Party and the government. People were filled with the exhilaration of release and relief and freedom to voice anger at what had befallen them. The new men still sitting far from securely in the seats of power had little choice but to let it run its course. For nearly two years, survivor stories filled the official press, piling horror on horror of the violence wreaked in Mao's name by Party members on Party members and hosts of others. Ordinary people, petitioners who came by the thousands from all over the country, virtually besieged government offices in Peking seeking redress from injustices they had suffered at the hands of arrogant bureaucrats. Demonstrators marched without leave, words of protest and criticism and demands for reform were spoken out loud, and were plastered in large and small characters in public places, most conspicuously toward the end of 1978, on Peking's "Democracy Wall"—readily accessible to foreign correspondents—and began to appear in both the official press and, more radically, in a sudden small eruption of illegal publications.

These demands eventually ran to the extreme of calling for the democratization of the whole Communist system, bringing on the first strong reassertion of limits by the new leadership in the spring of 1979. Some poster-writers and publishers of illegal journals were arrested—the most famous among them the youthful Wei Ching-sheng, of whose case more later—and the short-lived "Democracy Wall" was blanked out. It was all very well to move toward freeing the paralyzed economy and "modernizing," but freeing speech and political action was another matter and the new regime moved to choke off the spontaneous currents that began to move in that direction.

Still the spigot was not, and perhaps could not be, turned as rapidly as Mao Tse-tung, with Teng Hsiao-ping serving as his lieutenant, turned it in 1957 when he allowed the famous "Hundred Flowers" to bloom for a few months before ruthlessly cutting down the shoots that sprang up so swiftly and grew so fast in his Party garden. Now, in 1979-80, Teng and his friends sat at the top of a Party and government bureaucracy still heavily peopled by those appointed in Mao's (and Mrs. Mao's) time, deeply entrenched, still committed by conviction or association to the Maoist outlook, or at least too spotted with it to change very quickly. Many among them had actually committed the many crimes of the Cultural Revolution, that "mistake" of Mao's which one of the most senior figures in the new leadership finally denounced as "an appalling catastrophe suffered by all the people." The Maoist legacy in the regime was too strong to be rooted out too abruptly, its holders too numerous to purge, it was repeatedly pointed out, without causing more disruption than the regime could bear. To achieve "stability" the need was to compromise, temporize, not confront. The "criminals" would have to be punished but the "blind followers" would have to be treated more gently. On the other hand, the new leadership needed to deal with the formidable problems of the economy and the society by freeing them from the ideological shackles of Maoist leftism. To do this, the new leaders knew they would have to be looser, less rigid, less doctrinaire. But how to accomplish this without yielding up their own centralized control and power? How to be and at the same time not to be all-powerful, that was their question. Teng Hsiao-ping and his friends wanted to change things, but they had not come to preside over the liquidation of their Communist state. Some version of "Marxism-Leninism" was still their creed, even though Mao Tse-tung was no longer its prophet.

At the time of the encounters reported in these notes, the Party was engaged in a discussion aimed to achieve agreement on a document that would set down the new official view of the Party's history and Mao's role in it. No final formulation had been made. Individuals could speak their minds within uncertain limits, so uncertain that this subject—what one thought about Mao Tse-tung—was the only subject on which anyone asked me to be careful about the way I used what they said.

On Judging Mao

In the matter of judging Mao Tse-tung, more than one person

reminded me during our talks that Mao himself, writing twenty years ago at the time of "de-Stalinization" in Russia under Khrushchev, said that Stalin had been "30 percent wrong and 70 percent right." The question now being discussed in the Chinese Communist Party was what score to give Mao himself. The "cult of personality" which Mao had so sedulously cultivated had already been condemned by the Party. The super-heroic statues and pictures of Mao were coming down. But how far should "de-Maoization" go?

I did not nor was I likely to meet any unreconstructed Maoist who might have said, however injudiciously, that Mao had been "right" more than Stalin ever was, if not 100 percent "right" all of the time (as both Stalin and Mao always had to be while they reigned), then at least 90 percent most of the time. Those I did meet were all, like the new leaders, victims of what had gone "wrong" under Mao. But this did not mean that they would have opted for finding him 100 percent or even 90 percent "wrong." They all accepted the "line" which was that the Party had to reduce but not erase Mao's image as Great Leader, avoid any massive purge of Mao's people in the Party, government, and army, and amid the "stability" thus assured, go ahead with the effort to rescue the country from the ravages of Mao's rule. If what they did say in our talks were to be translated into percentages, I would guess they might have scored Mao as having been anywhere from 40 to 60, even to 80 percent "wrong," according to differences among them. It was precisely these differences that caught my attention early in these encounters, differences that had to do with how old they were, and the time and settings in which they had lived their political lives.

There was the outlook of Party veterans now sixty, like Fong Mu, the Writers Association official who welcomed us in Peking, who entered the Party around 1940, as the time of its greatest victories was just beginning, the years of Mao Tse-tung's most glitteringly successful leadership. The aura of it could not be dimmed without dimming what were for these veterans the best years of their lives.

But there were other veterans more veteran than they, now in their seventies, who joined the Party around 1930, ten years or so before the Fong Mus, in the time of the repression and terror of the regime of Chiang Kai-shek and the Kuomintang. More veteran still were those, now in their eighties, whose beginnings went all the way back to the beginnings of the Party itself, in the 1920s, and who experienced as youthful participants the sweeping rise and crashing fall of the revolutionary movement of those years. The differences between these older and younger veterans were made in these decade-long spaces between them, by the shape of things when they had first come in, by what they had experienced in these intensely different tightly compressed intervals of recent Chinese history.

Obviously, the varieties of personal experience were many in all of these years, but speaking only of the members of this seventies-eighties group whom I knew, the major difference between them and the sixty-year-old veterans I met on this journey was that the political roots of the older ones were in the prewar cities rather than in the wartime countryside. They had lived underground political lives under constant threat of imprisonment and death and they had known the numbing blows of loss and defeat at the hands of "class enemies" long before they suffered them again so much less bearably at the hands of their own comrades. It meant that they knew more about the Party's history, that they had some conception of the reality gap between the "proletarian leadership" the Communist Party always claimed it represented and the peasant-based force it actually became under Mao. They were contemporaries of Mao in the earlier years or had at least known other leadership styles. Their allegiance to the pre-eminent Mao was much less likely to be sicklied over by the pale cast of reverence. They were ever-faithful to the Party, even, like Mao Tun, rigid in the mold, but they were too old and too knowing to be romantic, much less worshipful, where Mao was concerned. They were better educated than their juniors if only because they had more time and opportunity to learn more about the diversity of peoples and societies and they had, in many cases—unlike Mao himself—a wider personal experience of the world. Several had been to Russia in earlier years and had seen what Stalin's regime looked like close up. They knew foreign languages, had traveled to Europe and America, or at least known Europeans and Americans in China. This greater breadth and awareness made them more sophisticated, less given to romantic illusions, more realistic, but perhaps more vulnerable thereby to cynicism.

By contrast, those who entered the political scene after 1938 knew nothing in their first years but hope, success, and victory during what might be called the golden age of Mao's leadership. They lived the hard life of wartime in the hinterlands but soon, sooner than most might have expected, they entered the cities with victorious armies and helped to create a new regime in which they had unbounded faith. But these were also young people who were likely to have had their education cut short by the turmoil of those years. They have lived ever since in a kind of tunnel. They were isolated during the war years and remained hardly less so when they came in from the countryside to serve as functionaries in the new order of things. Life under Mao offered little chance to widen one's horizon. Higher education was restricted and at best hemmed in by a numbingly pedantic elementary Marxism embellished by "Mao's Thoughts." Those who could meet foreigners had mostly only Russians and East European Communists to meet along with a small scatter of others. Contact with foreigners was not easy or encouraged in Mao's time—it is still limited. Few had any chance to go abroad, and those who did go on official missions apparently remained quite enclosed in their own physical or mental compounds. In any case, whatever chance there might have been for any kind of broadening during those first years of Communist power was soon cut off altogether for these victims of successive purges. Their lot from 1957 on was exile, imprisonment, and worse. This went on for twenty years during which hundreds of thousands of this generation of Party veterans who were in any way identifiable as "intellectuals" were buried, many of them quite literally, in the limbos created by Mao and his Gang of Four. Old and less old alike, all who re-emerged in 1977 and 1978 came back blinking out of the darkness of that long tunnel of years. For all of them, the new threshold from which they could begin to look out on the world was formidably high and hard to reach. For the older ones, there was the bitter awareness that their own best years were spent, but there was at least the level of greater knowledge and experience on which they could still try to stand for as long as they could. For the sixty-year-olds, the memory of the golden years of their youth was not much of a step from which to begin a new ascent, but it was the only one they had.

On the subject of judging Mao, these age differences showed up not in views of what the Party had to do now but rather in what was said about Mao, how it was said, the setting in which it was placed. Thus sixty-year-old Li Shin, our Writers Association host, a serious and earnest man who told us he "joined the Revolution in 1938." He went to Yenan, Mao's base in far-off Shensi. "I saw Chairman Mao and Chu Teh (commander of the Red Army). It was a 100 percent free world. We won victories over the Japanese and the Kuomintang. I had not thought the nation could be liberated in such a short time. The Party leadership was intelligent and correct. At that time, whatever you did at Mao's direction was always right, always successful." Like so many of his age and place, Li Shin had only seven years in which to enjoy the fruits of the Great Leader's victories. He had become an editor of a literary journal headed by Ting Ling, and he went down, not long after she did, in the massive "Anti-Rightist" purge of writers and intellectuals that began in 1957. In 1958 Li, a twenty-year Party veteran, was expelled. His wife divorced him. He was sent off with thousands of others, to spend the next twenty years in limbo, working at farm labor camps in the Chinese Gulag, first near Hankow, then near Canton. "We were called traitors. We knew that was wrong. But we did not dare say anything." In the years that followed, "production went down, schools were shut down, children were wandering, old cadres and intellectuals were in prison. How could this be right? But we did not dare to say anything." Now that he and the country had been liberated for a second time, this time from Mao and his Gang of Four, what Li had to say was: "I think we should admit that in his late years Mao committed some mistakes, as Stalin did in his late years." I could only marvel, appalled, at what he was willing to call "some mistakes" and at how ready he was to assign these "mistakes" to Mao's "late" years—they filled twenty-seven years of Mao's rule, they took away twenty of Li Shin's forty years since Yenan—and how utterly unknowing he had to be to do the same for Stalin.

Or Fong Mu: "Some people would negate Mao entirely because of the Cultural Revolution. I think this is dangerous. There is a difference between Mao and the Gang of Four. Mao had his own responsibility for them and we can only call them ambitious conspirators. But Chairman Mao is still a great revolutionary. I am sixty years old, I have taken part in the revolution for forty years, and from my experience I can only draw the conclusion that Mao was a great revolutionary even though he made mistakes, made people suffer, especially us, who are veterans.

But if we can't see things in a cool way, we will negate Mao. We must not take this road.''

Here, for contrast, is what an older veteran said: "Right now the whole Party is discussing the draft resolution on the merits and demerits of Mao. It is difficult to say what the final document will be. It is to be a sober summing up of the fate of so many people like me. But it is not to be treated sentimentally because it will serve as a guide for our future.'' I learned during this conversation that "sentimentally" meant with personal feeling, with emotion, which was to be avoided, as against hardheaded, impersonal, which was preferred. He went on to say that he did not expect the document to go as far in denouncing Mao as the Russian Party's twentieth Congress went in denouncing Stalin. "But Mao's image as liberator of the nation will be much reduced. He will be left there in his tomb, but his portraits will be removed. 'Maoism' and 'Mao's Thoughts' will be redefined. His merits up to 1957 will be stated, but his role after 1957 will be criticized.'' Whatever was useful in Mao's "Thoughts" would come to be seen "as more collective, not a matter of his personal genius.'' He paused, and with what I might call a sentimental gleam in his eyes, he added: "At least, he will be demoted from holiness.''

Another older man was sharp about Mao and his place in the minds of the faithful: "Mao was an old-style intellectual. He was very jealous of new-style intellectuals. The Cultural Revolution was his creation. We are not in for full de-Maoization. Not now, maybe in a few years from now (laughing), maybe not until after World War Three. People are peasant-minded, worship-minded. Our Party is a peasant party. Peasants are not like workers. They always take a worshiping attitude, they are superstitious. When you take their object of worship away from them, they feel lost, they don't know where they are. Pictures of Mao are still up because many people still take a worshipful attitude toward him.'' Stalin's pictures are down, he added, "but even now criticisms of Stalin are not published. For the same reasons, judgment of Mao cannot be (entirely) open.''

Stalin's place in this Chinese setting is oddly unclear. The huge portrait of Mao was still up there on the high Tienanmen wall. But the equally large picture of Stalin, along with those of Marx and Lenin, which had hung for years facing Mao's, had been taken down just two months before our visit. This had been done in accordance with the officially ordered dismantling of the cult of personality that had been so energetically fostered in Mao's time with portraits, great statues, adulation, and the elevation of "Mao's Thoughts" to the status of holy writ. Mao was to be venerated not only as the greatest of China's greats but also as one of the greats of the world revolution. Hence Marx and Lenin. But why Stalin?

Stalin had never been a hero of the Chinese revolution. In 1925-27 he wrecked it. In the 1930s, he assigned little importance to Mao's peasant armies. In 1935 Mao took over leadership of the Party without Stalin's leave. Stalin saw no chance that Mao's armies could win power in the 1940s, pressing Mao after Japan's defeat to make his peace again with Chiang Kai-shek whom he expected—and possibly even wanted—to regain power. In expectation that he would do so, Stalin used the Russian occupation of Manchuria to loot it of all usable industrial machinery, carting it all off to needy Russia. Why, I had long wondered, should any Chinese Communist venerate Stalin? I put the question to some of those I met on this journey.

One of my sixty-year-old acquaintances replied with characteristic simplicity: "Our Party decided we must not think of every great person as a god. Everyone has good points and bad points. That's what Mao said about Stalin and that's what we have to say for Chairman Mao now." I pressed briefly by citing some of the history involved. He wrestled with this for a moment or two and then came up again with a characteristic reply: "Stalin finally realized that Mao had always been right. And we, for our part, after Liberation, still thought the Soviet Union was the beacon of world revolution."

Older friends came up with varied but characteristically more substantial replies:

- Stalin's past history in relation to China had nothing to do with the case. Moscow was the only possible source of help in 1945 to defeat the U.S.-Kuomintang alliance in the civil war and later in rebuilding the country. "Mao went to Moscow in 1950 and got help, 160 building projects." Hence all honor to Stalin, ruler of Russia.

- After Stalin's death, Mao could not accept de-Stalinization, especially at the hands of Khrushchev, whom he thought of as an inferior figure. (At some deeper level, possibly, he saw Stalin as a mirror image of himself, the Great and Revered Leader. His cult in

China was not unlike Stalin's in Russia. The collapse of the one might have seemed to be like too much of an augury for the other.)

- Perhaps most persuasively, Mao was described as seeing himself as the crowning achiever in the development of the world revolution, as leader and as theoretician. He always indicated a belief in the continuity between himself and great rulers of China's past and also saw himself as representing continuity on a world scale, a world revolutionary continuity beginning with Marx and Engels, carried on in Russia by Lenin and Stalin, all invested with godhood in the western Communist world, and culminating in China with Mao Tse-tung. Any politics of passing moments were minor matters compared to this lofty image.

* * *

Postscript: The official judgment on Mao Tse-tung finally appeared in a document called "On Questions of Party History," issued in the name of the Central Committee on June 27, 1981. It met the need to strike a balance among differing interests by arriving at a remarkably lopsided imbalance between condemnation and praise of Mao.

It came down easy on the Anti-Rightist Campaign of 1957-58 (in which it happens that Teng Hsiao-ping was on Mao's side) calling it "entirely correct and necessary," regretting only that it was made "far too broad" with the result that "a number of intellectuals, patriotic people and Party cadres" suffered "unfortunate consequences." But it came down hard on the Cultural Revolution (of which it happens that Teng was a victim). It was "a catastrophe to the Party, the state, and the whole people." It was "initiated and led by Comrade Mao Tse-tung." Its worst crimes, however, the document quickly went on to say, were committed "behind his back" by counter-revolutionary cliques "taking advantage of Comrade Mao's errors, bringing disaster to the country and the people." But as these "crimes have been fully exposed, this resolution will not go into them at any length." Mao "confused right and wrong and the people with the enemy during the 'cultural revolution,'" it went on, "but after all this was the error of a great proletarian revolutionary" looked on by the people as "their respected and beloved great leader and teacher."

In sum: "Comrade Mao Tse-tung was a great Marxist and a great proletarian revolutionary, strategist, and theorist. It is true that he made gross mistakes during the 'cultural revolution,' but if we judge his activities as a whole, his contributions to the Chinese revolution far outweigh his mistakes. His merits are primary and his errors secondary."

In a word, 30 percent "wrong" and 70 percent "right."

* * *

To all this, finally, I must add a further postscript of my own. (As to age group, just to be clear, I am at this writing seventy-three.) There is a paradox that threads its way through this history, ironic enough in almost any view, but indescribably so for anyone who shared in whatever degree in these experiences. I can only guess what these onetime Chinese Communist friends of mine would make of it.

Mao Tse-tung's leadership of the Chinese Communist Party was kindled in the disaster that Stalin so largely made in 1927 because he, Stalin, held what was essentially a national-Communist view of revolutionary struggles in other countries. He saw them as subject to the supreme need to serve Russia's interests, translated for purposes of rationalization into the need to defend the world's only so-called workers' state. Trotsky fought Stalin's course in China, opposing Stalin's view of the "stages" of the revolution with the argument that only the "proletariat" could successfully lead the revolution to its conclusion. He confronted Stalin's nationalist formula of subordinating everything to the building of "socialism in one country" with what Trotsky saw as an uncompromisingly Leninist "proletarian" internationalism. Eventually—twenty-two years after the 1927 defeat—Mao Tse-tung led the Chinese Communists to power without benefit either of Stalin's mechanical "stage" theory of revolution or Trotsky's puristic proletarianism. He did it by the distinctly non-Leninist strategy of sweeping in on the cities from the hinterland with Communist-led peasant armies, preserving the necessary doctrinal purity by simply identifying the Communist Party with the "proletariat." In power, Mao became in his turn the greatest national-Communist of them all, breaking with post-Stalin Russia to follow his own course and calling upon the world Communist movement to recognize Peking, not

Moscow, as the center of true revolutionism.

But—and here the ironic twist becomes a dizzy spiral—the banner under which Mao summoned the world to follow him, from a Peking still adorned with Stalin's portraits years after Stalin's posthumous downfall, was inscribed with a close replica of Trotsky's device of the "permanent revolution." In Mao's version it was called the "continuous revolution." Trotsky's "permanent revolution" was the relentless advance of the working class through and past the temporary tenure of the bourgeoisie toward "the victory of socialism" in each country, in country after country until it encompassed the entire globe. Mao's "continuous revolution" was something that went on and had to go on within the Communist Party itself, especially the victorious Party, ever prone to being recaptured by the insidious forces and ideas of the bourgeoisie, the class enemy with a thousand lives, and therefore subject to constant vigilance and correction, a constant peeling off of its outer skin and a renewal from within, only thereby assuring its vigor and purity and unalloyed dedication to the making over not only of society but of man himself. Here was dialectic with a marvelous vengeance: Leninism producing Stalinism versus Trotskyism fusing into a super-revolutionary Maoism which has now lost out to its antithesis (reality? pragmatism?) beginning to produce we still know not what. It waits on what the next political generation makes of it.

A Further Generational Note

Describing the elders of the revolution, I have made much of the matter of where and when they came in, the view of politics and the world they acquired from the scene as they entered it. What can be said of those who came after them? How about all those younger than our aging and aged veterans? What notions of all this history, what images of Mao, what definitions of "revolution," what sense of themselves, of the country, of the world, what of all this has been printed on their minds by events experienced since *they* came in?

What can be said of those now in their forties and fifties who reached their places in the system in Mao's years and were in great numbers the actual criminal perpetrators, the "blind followers," or passive onlookers, makers of the catastrophe? Of those now in their thirties who swarmed to join the "Red Guards" licensed by Mao himself to beat and kill, to commit violence on their elders, to wreck, vandalize, destroy, to attack Party and government offices, universities, schools, private homes, all in the name of doing away with "enemies of the people"? Of all those city youngsters, twenty to thirty now, who rotted away in the countryside to which they had been sent, or wandered loose for ten years while all schools were closed, and who now work at low-level labor from which they have no chance of rising, or else simply molder as part of the huge army of youthful unemployed that burdens China's dragging economy? Or join the growing numbers of youthful criminals preying on the system at all its ragged edges?

These are formidable questions for those concerned with how—or whether—a viable regime can be created in Communist China. They open a large subject waiting for much more than its authors: it waits just around the corner of near time to become the key to the shape of things in China's next oncoming political generation. It was certainly not waiting for this author who with two weeks in which to learn something about the experience of a small number of older veterans of this history could hardly have attempted to explore these further questions about the young. Here again, I can contribute only a few gleanings as they turned up in the talks we had with the sixty-seventy-eighty-year-olds we met.

* * *

"There are many younger people who only got into politics when the Cultural Revolution began. In their minds is the thought that making a 'revolution' is what they saw and did in the Cultural Revolution. They knew very little about our struggle and our history before and after Liberation. They are disappointed in the revolution and the Party. I am talking about those who are now thirty to forty, including many who took part as Red Guards. Some have drawn lessons from it and now realize the actions of the Cultural Revolution were wrong. But some are puzzled, confused, some still support the ideas of the Cultural Revolution. They say the Gang of Four were not so bad, what they did was not so bad. After all, they benefited from it."

* * *

"I see four groups. First, veterans like myself—though I can't speak of all veterans, we have agreements and disagreements among us on these matters; second, young people who are disappointed; third, those young and not so young who still are pro-Cultural Revolution; and fourth, most important, those, both young and middle-aged, who do not take a simple view, who are thinking about the problems. They are what we call the 'thoughtful generation,' those who now realize they were deceived in the Cultural Revolution, that it was not an isolated phenomenon but was connected to what had gone on before, that not only was the Cultural Revolution wrong but that some things were wrong *before* the Cultural Revolution. They see that there is much to do, that we must be responsible and do the job, that we have to think hard about how to cure our country of this disgrace."

* * *

"There are three age groups. The oldest, those who participated early in the revolution, are for the most part not in responsible positions. A few are very high, but eight out of ten of them are in the military, not in civilian positions. But those who are in high positions, military or not, become part of a feudal bureaucracy, bureaucrats who forget the people entirely. At the beginning, people were paid in kind, then in wages. But high officials were paid both in money *and* in kind: housing, food, attendants, all copied from Russia. They get privileges, they get out of touch with the public, they get callous to people's suffering and welfare. They have special shops with provisions for themselves, just like in Russia, fish, meat, wine. Right here on this street every morning cars line up to pick up supplies for high civilian and military officials. And the same is done in every provincial capital.

"The second group, in the fifty-sixty age group, has many intelligent, hard-working people doing routine work. They can't express themselves. They do their duty. They are handicapped by the system. It is a split system, split between those who manage the work and those who manage the placing of people. Those who manage the work, god bless them, can't get good people to do the work. There is a separation of ability and authority that is a fundamental problem. All are handicapped by this, everybody, and there is no change in this so far.

"A third group, thirties to fifties, are largely cynical, pessimistic. Among the youngest, the fourth group, there is also a division, some very clearheaded, they want to study, work, pass exams. Others are criminals and rascals."

* * *

"I can tell you about a young man who is twenty-four. He comes to see us with his friends. They are young workers who lost any chance to go to senior middle school. They got through three years of junior middle school, then the Cultural Revolution closed all the schools, there was no chance. He would have been sent to the countryside like all the others, but because he was an only child, he was exempted. He became a worker. He doesn't like to read serious things or listen to the news. He tries to get tickets for western movies. He listens to tapes of western pop music. In the short period when social dancing was allowed, he danced. That is now forbidden. He has long hair. He wanted to wear jeans. His mother ordered him not to. When I talked to him about affairs, he would say: what's the use, one thing then, another thing now, and so on. A kind of strong skepticism. He works in an automobile factory, but he is not fond of his work. It is work he does because he has to do it. He is quite typical. There are several types, some very bad, with a strong impact of Cultural Revolution rebelliousness. They now lack confidence in any authority. They will take any chances. There is much juvenile crime, robbing, raping. There had to be a campaign mounted against it."

* * *

"[The criminals of the Cultural Revolution] were young people mostly, up to about thirty. Chairman Mao thought the old cadres represented the bourgeois class and that the Party needed to be punished. Young people and blind followers did this. Some of the young generation now know how much the older cadres and older generals did for the revolution, how much they need to be respected and they see how puerile and childlike and stupid some younger people were. Our leaders for ten years from now have to be re-educated. We strongly believe now that no absolute power should be given to any leader. Not only we older ones think this, but most of the young think the same way, for more democratization, more liberalism.''

The Limits

How much ''democratization''? How much ''liberalism''? Where were the limits *now?* These questions hovered close over all our conversations: what could be said now, what could be written, even thought? Anger and pain could still be expressed about what was past but in this as in everything else, it was necessary to stay within the limits of the evolving ''line'' of the new leadership; only once or twice did anyone stray very far beyond it, even if only with a wayward phrase. There was obviously a mix of reasons why this was so. It was not hard to subscribe to a writ that had restored one to life. It was also a matter of a well-learned reflex of caution, of looking over one's shoulder in a situation where particular questions of people and power and outlook were still unsettled. It was also a matter of still believing that the Party was all, that only its inner health and truth had caused it to veer off just in time from the road to disaster and take a turn that would save it and save the country, as indeed it had saved them and given them the chance to make their own last years count for something in the process. As to the despair they must have felt, the despairing had died, these were survivors who would not yield up their faith no matter how ghostly it had become.

In any case, for writers it was far more than a matter of what they might say to a visitor reappearing out of the distant past who came to them asking troubling questions. It was more a matter of what they would or would not write now about themselves, about all that had happened to them and to so many others, whether in memoirs or behind the screen of fiction. Speaking only of those I met, it was clear that caution reigned. Mao Tun said he would write of his life only up to 1949 and I do not know if he had reached even that far when he died a few months after we talked. Ting Ling, seventy-seven and ailing, said she was writing a novel ''about peasants'' and brushed away as unseemly the notion that she ought to be writing about herself instead, only finally promising, sort of, that she would turn to herself as subject, but not until she had done with her peasants. In Shanghai similar exchanges ended similarly, though not without an intimation that some such writing might yet get done. Someone mentioned the excerpts that had appeared from memoirs written by Peng Teh-huai, the military leader who rose high in the heroic days when all he had to face were Chiang Kai-shek's troops and the Japanese, but fell victim early, in 1959, in the experience of facing his own fellow-Communist leaders. What he had written had remained long hidden. "Only a small part of it has been published," one of those present said. "But it will be, it will be, you'll see. It is a matter of time. They will write, they will *all* write."

*   *   *

Over many years, the violence of the politics into which they were drawn has had a way of cutting down Chinese writers before they had the chance to realize their gifts to any fullness. Writers were among the principal targets of all the forms of terror and repression that doomed so many to die or rot in the time of the Kuomintang or in the Communist years since. The Communist constraints—years of stultifying labor, confinement, remote exile, imprisonment—were by far the more difficult to bear; they lasted longer and they came at the hands not of the hated foe but of the Party of Liberation itself. The evidence is that out of fear or despair or both, many stopped writing altogether for many years and some might now find it too late or too difficult to resume. Where younger writers stand now in post-Mao China is another large subject I could not explore and to which I can contribute only a glimpse or two as they appeared in talks we had during this brief journey. It took no great exploration, however, to see that while the shackles of "anti-Rightism" and the Cultural Revolution had been struck away by the change in leadership, the new dispensation was still a long way from Liberation for anyone in China who wanted to write, paint, or film as he or she felt moved to do. In these, as in all related matters, the time of our visit was a time of passage between differing measures of constraint. Insofar as there was any relatively greater freedom at the moment—as in the "horror stories" of the Cultural Revolution—no one could be sure how long it would last. The limits might be shifted from where they stood in Mao's time, but there could be no illusions about the uncertainties of the moment. Nothing resembling freedom of expression was about to come into view.

Thus Fong Mu, the vice-chairman of the Writers Association, told us that there was some greater freedom for writers to write. "It is just beginning, in stories and novelettes. But"—he immediately added—"but it is difficult to achieve freedom for the writer to write everything. There are still many stumbling blocks in the way of freedom of writers in their work of creation. But I am optimistic about writers, about their courage and sensibility. It is less difficult now for short stories, easier to get them published. There are no censors; editors have the right to publish or not publish."

And what were the blocks? "An interesting phenomenon. The Chinese Writers Association decides the fate of literary work that is submitted. The people in the Association are writers themselves, so they take correct attitudes about this literature, so generally speaking short stories, novelettes, poems, are judged for themselves. But a film or play will be checked very carefully. This is because new short stories and poems are published directly by mass organizations like the Writers Association [meaning one thin cut away from direct governmental or Party control] but films and plays go through the Ministry of Culture and its bureaucracy, and there it is different."

But then Fong Mu himself went on to illustrate the wide gap between the free writer and the controlling bureaucrat sanctioned by a governing ideology.

"No government official should interfere with literary creation or give orders," he said. "But this is a goal difficult to achieve. As a leading member of the Writers Association, I uphold the idea that writers who serve the people and social construction have the greatest possible freedom." And there was the rub; for those who remained within these officially defined limits, "the greatest possible freedom," but for those who did not, obviously, there could be no freedom at all. I do not know how many new young writers, like painters we did hear about, are venturing on their own out into that dangerous territory beyond the barriers; one waits to hear about them. What was clear enough in any case was that the political changes in process brought with them the beginning of a new struggle between writers and Party bureaucrats, an old and much fought-over battleground in the Chinese Communist Party where writers have never won.

* * *

In the arena not of literary but of political free expression, the new limits had already been plainly set for anyone who carried the idea of any new "freedom" too far. This occurred in the case of twenty-nine-year-old Wei Ching-sheng who became the best-known of some remarkable young people who entered the world of politics as Red Guards in their 'teens in 1966 and emerged from that experience as boldly challenging critics of the lack of humanism and democracy in the Communist regime. Much writing in this spirit appeared through 1978 and half of 1979 in underground journals and on posters put up in public places—a form of public expression specifically granted in the new 1978 Constitution—of which the most famous became Peking's "Democracy Wall." Here on the street Wei Ching-sheng and his friends openly sold their journal *Exploration* and discussed these issues with the crowd that clustered there every day, including foreign correspondents who told the whole world about it. In April 1979, police began to pull down and destroy posters hung on "Democracy Wall." Wei Ching-sheng, who had put up what became his most famous article, "The Fifth Moderniza-tion—Democracy and Related Topics," was arrested. He was tried in October 1979 on charges of "counter-revolutionary crimes" and betrayal of "military secrets" to foreigners—because he had discussed with correspondents at the Wall China's unsuccessful border attack on Vietnam in February 1979—and was sentenced to fifteen years' imprisonment. In December, the government abolished "Democracy Wall" altogether, relegating all poster-hanging to a more remote place and then only after advance of-ficial scrutiny of what was going up. Shortly thereafter, in January 1980, Teng Hsiao-ping personally announced that the clause granting the right to hang wall posters would be excised from the new Constitution. Much has been written about these cir-cumstances and the case of Wei Ching-sheng but to give some idea of the tone and substance of this reassertion of ideas re-surfacing in China after so many years of submergence, I quote here one paragraph from Wei's own statement in his defence during his trial, smuggled out of the country and widely published abroad:

> The current revolutionary tide is the tide of democracy. It is the tide of opposing feudal, fascist dictatorship and despotism. The evolution of Chinese society suggests to the Chinese people that unless the social system is reformed and the root of dictatorial and fascist despotism is thoroughly removed, unless democracy is practiced and the people's democratic rights are protected, Chinese society will not be able to move forward and socialist modernization cannot be realized. . . . The central theme of my articles, such as "The Fifth Modernization—Democracy and Related Topics" is that if there is no democracy, there will be no four modernizations, and that without the fifth modernization—democracy—all the rhetoric about modernization is just a new lie. How can such a central theme be regarded as counter-revolutionary? (Quoted in Ta-ling Lee and Miriam London, "Wei Ching-sheng Defends Himself," *Freedom at Issue,* May/June 1980, no. 56.)

At his trial, the prosecutor said:

> Our Constitution clearly stipulates extensive democratic rights. . . . It does not mean absolute freedom for one to do as one likes. . . . Freedom of speech of the individual citizen must be based on the four basic principles of insisting on the socialist road, the dictatorship of the proletariat, and Marxism-Leninism-Mao Tse-tung Thought. The citizen has only the freedom to support these principles, not to oppose them. . . ." (Quoted by Jonathan Spence, *The Gate of Heavenly Peace,* New York, 1981, p. 363.)

I cite these matters here because they came up in my conversation with Fong Mu when he said: "Our country will be helpless if it takes the way of dictatorship, rule by orders, against democracy—our country cannot suffer from this again." How then, I asked him, was one to understand the case of Wei Ching-sheng? With this question, I abruptly ran into a limit myself, a palpable limit. Fong Mu, who had been talking steadily and readily and authoritatively in response to all other questions, pulled back sharply, his easy flow of speech suddenly interrupted, the clear "line" of his answers suddenly muddied. What he came up with was an attack on Wei Ching-sheng. "He does not belong to what I have called 'the thoughtful generation.' He is not a hero as foreigners think. Foreigners called him a writer, but he's not worthy of being called a writer. He didn't have a glorious idea, much of his point of view is rejected by the people. . . . He rejected our leaders completely, especially in slogans, concentrating on Teng Hsiao-ping. The people thought that was totally wrong."

But why such a heavy sentence, I asked, when all he did was put a paper up on a wall? At this, Fong Mu pulled back even more. After a pause, he said: "I don't know, I didn't read the details of his trial. Some people are discussing this problem too. As to his punishment, that was for the people in the court to say. Some of his ideas are not good, so many that the Chinese people do not like. And to get money he exposed military secrets to foreigners. He jeopardized the law. I don't think his case has to do with freedom for writers to write—that is with past history. The main stumbling block for writers now is our bureaucratic style." I pressed a little about those "military secrets" but Fong drew back from the question. "This is beyond my ability to say. I know very little about it."

This exchange was one to ponder, all the more when something very like it happened again a few days later in a conversation with Liu Pin-yen, a well-known writer-journalist who had spoken out in his own way on some of the most sensitive issues that were newly aired during this relatively open time. The Chinese writer, I thought, was going through an opening and a closing, something like a whale surfacing for air before submerging again to the airless dark below.

*   *   *

Liu Pin-yen, also a survivor of exile and imprisonment, presented a lively picture of what it felt like out on the surface at this moment in Chinese journalism. An exuberant, self-assured man in his late fifties, author of short stories and essays, in our conversation Liu spoke of himself and presented his views primarily as a writer for the *People's Daily,* the regime's principal newspaper. In this role he had recently achieved fame as an exposer of corruption in high places, higher than had ever been exposed in this fashion before; he brought down an important government minister who had put his hand too deeply and too often in the public till. He spoke as a man who believed that an increasingly free-wheeling press, hand in hand with the enlightened masses, would be able to put things to right in troubled China where so much was still wrong.

"It is a golden time for newsmen in China now!" he zestfully announced. Golden? "Yes, golden, because it is a time of revising, of changing, a very dramatic time." How much leeway do you have? "For thirty years," he replied, "our newspapers have published only good news, not bad news, praise, not criticism. Now that is changing. Now we are allowed to criticize. We are getting the freedom to explore, to investigate." But getting such material published, he went on, remains a problem. They are managing now, he explained, through a two-tier system, the regular newspaper for the whole public—circulation 7 million—and a special supplement for insiders only, he could not or would not say how many. "We have closed material, a classified section which is printed but is read by Party members only, by cadres. It carries the name *People's Daily* but it is not made up like a newspaper although the items in it all carry the names of the reporters who write them. Some of this material eventually does get into the regular paper, the rest does not, being thought not proper to tell the world or the Chinese people."

Who decides? "The editors of the newspaper decide. It is often a matter of choosing when to publish something. But there are great changes. Newspapers now supply much more news than they did before. This is a great change. It used to be said, in the matter of criticism, that 'we hit flies, never the tiger.' But this has changed too. We used to be careful where ministers and provincial officials were involved, but not now."

And what *is* sacred now? "The needs of the people, the interest of the people. Things are complicated in China now. We must seize the right time to do some things. Take the question of Mao, we are going to judge him openly. We couldn't have done this three or four years ago. Now is the right time. Until 1975, I respected Chairman Mao very much, even though I was a 'rightist' in 1957. In 1969, I would have carried a copy of 'Mao's Thoughts' myself to Tienanmen Square. I was forty-four then. But we are awakened now. The Cultural Revolution was not in vain because it wakened the people and we can now judge Chairman Mao."

The people? "Yes, a great many people who have come to realize the mistakes of the last twenty years. It was impossible before, it is possible now. Yes, I mean people in the streets, and not just here in Beijing but in other cities, and in all kinds of varying degrees." How do you know about the people? "We get letters, thousands of letters. And we are just beginning to take some opinion polls." Isn't it difficult to get people to give opinions to pollers from a government paper? "Yes, but in many universities there are many now who dare to speak their views. Recently a magazine opened a public discussion on the subject of why life's path for people is so narrow. They got 10,000 letters full of comments and ideas about the Party, the government, the society! Many of these letters are now being published in that magazine, which has a circulation of two million."

"I have no doubt"—he raced on—"that the leadership has now adopted a correct policy to change China. Teng Hsiao-ping has taken many measures. How to translate these into reality is a difficult problem, to try to revise the economic system, to revise the political system. I think it is easier to change the economic system than to change the political system. I mean improve it," he added hastily, "not change it altogether."

"I think we need a strong constitution and firm leaders who carry it out in earnest. In some people's minds, the idea of a constitution is not very strong. I think a constitution is important, but I also understand that it cannot solve all the problems because of the special position of the Communist Party. So our problem is to remold it to make it a better Party. The Party must control itself. Things are wrong in the Party, not only in the mind but in the body of the Party. The changes needed have to do with how the Party should lead the country, how the government should rule the country. The vital thing is to have democracy, to give the people rights."

And this, he said, was beginning to happen, with some factories adopting their own profit-sharing plans, with workers beginning to elect their own group leaders and managers, and an experimental plan in which *hsien* or county heads would be elected instead of appointed. This is being tried, he said, in 1,200, or half the districts in the country. "It will be done in all districts," Liu said, "according to the decisions already taken. The trouble is that people don't know how to use their rights. They are concerned with having enough food, not with politics. They are poorly educated, narrow-minded. If they get to have a better life, a higher standard of living, they will do better in politics. Politics and economics depend on each other. I am optimistic about the future. Though we have moved late, we are better off than in the Soviet Union or Eastern

Europe, except for Yugoslavia. We are doing away with permanent leadership. We are the first socialist country to do this, we are talking about fixing terms for office, perhaps four or five years.''

How about the spigot, I asked, it was turned on in 1957 and turned off—won't this happen again? ''Intellectuals are worried about this,'' Liu replied. ''But now nobody can close the spigot. This sluice gate is open. Nobody can close it. People have a bowl of rice in their hands; they won't allow anyone to take it away. For intellectuals, this bowl of rice means freedom. Now in 1980 there are some people who would like to close the spigot. But they dare not do it openly. They can only spread rumors behind people's backs and wait their chance. But my view is that they will lose this chance forever by 1985.''

How then, I asked, about Wei Ching-sheng? Here once more, it was as though I had closed a spigot myself. Liu Pin-yen had been talking in a steady flow, rapid and full of excitement, full of command of what he thought and what he was saying. He had been leaning forward intently giving me his bright view of what was going on, of the promise it offered for the future. My question stopped him short. He leaned back in his chair and when his answer came, it came slowly, almost haltingly. ''I am not clear about the Wei Ching-sheng matter,'' he said. ''I know very little about it. I wasn't here in Beijing then.'' His expression had gone flat. He stopped and lit a cigarette. ''I think many of my answers already answer your question, but indirectly,'' he said. I started to ask him to explain what he meant but he went on past my further question. ''I really don't know the details of that case,'' he said flatly. ''I don't know why the trial took place. It is difficult to say. There is much that is still unfair. We are improving—'' and here he switched to another subject—''Many people are coming here to make complaints about things that should be solved in their provinces. They should not have to come so far so many times, but even when leading officials write from here to those in the provinces to solve these problems, they don't do so. . . .''

He looked at his watch, our time was gone, he had to leave, he said. We shook hands and parted. Various people whom we had asked had indicated that it was hard to know just where the new limits were, but we knew now where one big limit stood. It was at the line Wei Ching-sheng had crossed.

Postscript:

The Chinese Communist Party Central Committee has recently issued "Document No. 7" which calls for tightening the control over literary and artistic creations. The stipulations of the document forbid writing on the "anti-rightist struggle" and the "Cultural Revolution." . . . The first article in the February issue of *Wen Yi Pao* was "Literature and Art Must Uplift the Morale of the New Era." (*Chen Ming,* Hong Kong, March 1, 1981)

* * *

Peking—With great fanfare the Chinese Government last year began holding what it said were the first free and democratic county-level elections since the Communists came to power in 1949. . . . By the end of the year, about 70 percent of the counties had held "real democratic elections," Cheng Zihua, Minister of Civil Affairs, declared two weeks ago. But, he told a session of the National People's Congress Standing Committee, there were difficulties. Some people "with a desire to stir up trouble everywhere" had misinterpreted free elections to mean they could campaign against the Community Party . . . adding that "such anarchism and extreme individualism" was nothing but an effort to "destroy stability and unity." The elections would continue, he said, but with last year's "errors" corrected—meaning that the voting would be less free. (*New York Times,* March 22, 1981)

* * *

Peking, August 28 (Reuters)—Wang Renzhong, a high-ranking Communist Party official, has called for public criticism of Chinese authors and editors who believe that they should have more freedom to write and publish what they like. . . . "Problems of bourgeois liberalization are quite serious among some comrades," Mr. Wang was quoted as having said. "Such comrades included not only non-party people but also authors who are party members, some editors and deputy editors of publications." . . . The commentary charged that some recently published works had "distorted the party's image, defamed the socialist motherland and slandered Marxism-Leninism and Mao Zedong Thought." While it said that the bitter Maoist-style campaigns against authors in the past should not be repeated, it was necessary to carry out "real criticism and struggle" against mistaken tendencies. (*New York Times,* August 29, 1981)

* * *

Peking, September 17 (Reuters)—A Chinese dissident has smuggled out of the prison camp where he is held a document that provides an account of life in the penal camps where prisoners receive "education through labor."

"In the 196-page handwritten document, the dissident, Liu Qing [a co-founder of the unofficial magazine *April Fifth Forum* which ceased publication early in 1980] . . . the 38-year-old Mr. Liu . . . says he was beaten . . . , forced to wear manacles and held in solitary confinement for five months before being transferred to the Lotus Flower Temple labor camp [the *Lotus Flower Temple* labor camp!] in the northwestern province of Shaanxi. Mr. Liu was arrested in Peking in November 1979 after he sold transcripts of the trial of China's best-known dissident, Wei Jing-sheng. . . . " (*New York Times,* September 18, 1981)

* * *

Peking, September 29—The Communist Party chose the occasion of the centennial of the birth of one of China's greatest 20th century writers, Lu Hsun, to warn the country's writers that it will brook no opposition to its rule and tolerate no criticism of its dictates.

In the party's sharpest attack on free expression and dissent since China's present leadership assumed power, Hu Yaobang, the party chairman, railed against the "bourgeois liberalism" and "pernicious writing" that he said cast doubt on the supreme virtues of communism and socialism. . . .

Mr. Hu warned against those writers and artists who, he said, had an ingrained hatred for new China, socialism, and our party. "We must punish them by law for their counter-revolutionary activities," he said. . . . *The People's Daily* reinforced Mr. Hu's speech by admonishing writers and artists "to keep in step with the party," adding, "We must guard against and fight the tendency of bourgeois liberalism, or attempts to break away from leadership by the Communist Party and the socialist road."

Chinese intellectuals . . . were buoyed by the lessening of ideological constraints in 1978 by Mr. Deng [Teng Hsiao-ping]. . . . A small democracy movement was fostered, but some Chinese writers now accuse Mr. Deng of using them temporarily for his own political ends. Now that his enemies in power have been purged and his proteges have been elevated to positions as head of the party and head of the government, these writers argue, Mr. Deng has succumbed to traditional tactics for stifling critics." (*New York Times,* September 30, 1981)

* * *

CANTON

We had only a few hours in Canton en route to Hong Kong and home. We were put up for the night at a super-VIP guest house, a palace of vast rooms built, it was said, by a militarist who once ruled this city, but if so, patterned on a European idea of where the lords and ladies of creation were meant to sleep when they came to the far reaches of their realms. One approached bedroom, bath, and toilet along corridor space wide enough for a court procession. The bedroom, with mosquito nets curled high into cones up to a 20-foot ceiling, was large enough to hold audience in, and the bathroom large enough for a council hardly less privy. The furniture and fixtures were all strictly turn-of-century and there was not a single comfortable place to sit or light to read by. We did not know what entitled us to this worn opulence. Canton's hotels were said to be jammed with businessmen attending the trade fair, but this place was almost empty. We glimpsed only three or four other foreigners in the morning at a most unregal breakfast.

I had never been to this cradle of China's revolutions. It was from this part of the country that the Taipings moved north more than a hundred years ago to challenge the Manchu emperor. It was here that Sun Yat-sen launched the movement that toppled the empire in 1911 and it was here that the great risings of 1924-27 began. It was also in this city, less than a hundred miles upriver from the China Sea, that China's experience with encroaching foreign traders and invaders began about two centuries ago. We drove through the island of Shameen, the area of foreign concessions established by the treaty that ended the Opium War of 1840, down its tree-shaded streets still lined by palatial homes and buildings in the colonial style of the last century. It was on one of the bridges connecting Shameen to the rest of the city that the era of foreign domination also came to the beginning of its end one day in June 1925 when British and French machine gunners fired on a demonstration approaching from the city and killed fifty-two students, unionists, and military cadets. This came only three weeks after British police had similarly killed twelve students in Shanghai on May 30, touching off a general strike to paralyze that great northern metropolis. Now the same happened here, an anti-British boycott and general strike that immobilized all traffic downriver from Canton and the great British port of Hong Kong, seventy miles away at the Pearl River's mouth. Hong Kong remained paralyzed for nearly two years while the revolutionary movement swept northward, with Chiang Kai-shek riding its crest until April 12, 1927, when he turned on his Communist allies in his coup at Shanghai. A massive slaughter went on there and across the entire Yangtze Valley while he set up his own Kuomintang government at Nanking. The Communists, who had been submitting to Chiang's command at Stalin's explicit direction, were now ordered to react with a series of hopeless uprisings.

I recite this history because the largest of these uprisings was mounted in December 1927 here in Canton where the Communists no longer had any mass following, only a few thousand faithful militants surrounded by overwhelmingly superior forces of militarists again on their own or loosely allied to Chiang Kai-shek. These forces turned on the insurrectionists with thoroughgoing ferocity. The slaughter in Canton streets during those three December days filled the streets with nearly 6,000 dead. Under a photograph showing the corpses being piled into wagons, a Shanghai newspaper captioned: "The bodies of the dead were collected as so much cordwood and carted away for burial in a common grave."

Unlike Chiang Kai-shek's victims in Shanghai, these dead were remembered by the Communist regime with a monument of their own. With only an hour left to spend in Canton, we asked to be taken there. It was a tall column standing in a wide space of trees and walks and plantings called "Martyrs Park," filled on this sunny Sunday mid-morning with crowds of strollers. On the column was inscribed one of Mao's Thoughts about the revolution advancing from defeat to victory. I looked around at the small cluster of Writers Association hosts who were accompanying us. Did they know, I asked, what had taken place here? Yes, of course, they nodded, but apprehension creased Li Shin's face as Ho Pin translated what I had asked. He had grown to know how disquieting some of my questions could be. Yes, he answered readily. This was "an uprising that failed, but the revolution went on and Chingkangshan did not fail"—Chingkangshan was the mountain in Kiangsi where Mao and Chu Teh reassembled a tiny force of survivors in late 1927 and began all over again. But did they know, I persisted, what these martyrs were martyrs to, sacrificed by whom to what? Blank looks again, apprehension again on Li Shin's face. Standing there in the sunlight next to the stone shaft, I began to tell them, like a guide at an historic spot telling his audience more than they wanted to know about the history that rested there in this ground.

I told them how at the end of 1927, with the revolution shattered everywhere and thousands still being slaughtered by Chiang Kai-shek—Stalin's chosen instrument only a few months earlier—and his militarist allies across the country, some sign of revolutionary life was badly needed by Stalin in Moscow where the Fifteenth Congress of the Communist Party was to meet on December 15. So although many small uprisings had "failed" one after another since August, a new one was ordered up for Canton where it would be visible to the whole world and especially to the delegates at Stalin's Congress, proof that Stalin's crushed revolution was still alive, his "revolutionary wave" still rising. A Comintern specialist, a German named Heinz Neumann, was sent to Canton to organize the event and a date was set, not coincidentally, for just five days before the Moscow meeting. Neumann (executed by Stalin a few years later) had only a few remnants of the Party and Canton-Hong Kong strike pickets to command. There was no longer any sign of the massive workers' movement that had kept the British at bay in Hong Kong for so long; indeed, seamen and other waterfront workers, unaware of what was afoot, helped bring additional Canton militarist forces into the city to join the alert against the coming attempt. On December 10, Neumann's poorly armed insurrectionists went out into the streets to carry out his plan of attack. The idea was that their bold appearance would rally all those masses around them once more. But they stayed alive only long enough to proclaim the "Canton Commune" before being systematically wiped out by alerted troops waiting for them to appear. There had been no chance at all that this "uprising" would not fail, I told my little audience. They were martyrs not to the revolution but to Stalin who needed a sign, if only for a few days, that the Chinese revolution was still going on. Not one of those martyrs need have died.*

I stopped talking. My listeners looked embarrassed by my words and even more so, probably, by the passion with which they were spoken. The old anger and revulsion had risen in me again. Li Shin offered a small remonstrance. All revolutions have their defeats, he said, and ours, after all, did go on to victory. What a sometime thing, I thought, is history.

We had to hurry to the station to catch our train. Only Chinese with special permits were allowed to enter the area from which the Hong Kong train departed. Until recently, trains from Canton had gone only as far as the Hong Kong border, where passengers took themselves and their baggage across a bridge to board the Hong Kong train on the other side. But this train, reserved for foreigners only, was now a through train and only a few authorized Chinese could pass the barrier to the track that led to the outside world. All others, even porters, were barred. Li Shin and Ho Pin, our conscientious hosts who had looked after us with such care and dealt so stoically with my questions, insisted on carrying our bags themselves into the shed for customs inspection, then to the waiting room filled with several hundred foreign travelers, and finally on to the train itself. They left us at our seats, accepted our thanks, bade us goodbye, and then stood outside on the platform at our window to wave farewell as we pulled out.

*For documentation see *The Tragedy of the Chinese Revolution,* 2nd rev. ed. 1961, Stanford University Press, Chap. 17. In Chinese Communist history, the event barely gets a line, even if it did get a monument in Canton.

A NOTE ON SOME READINGS

Here are some suggested readings for the reader who seeks further information on the figures and events mentioned in this book:

For studies of Lu Hsun and other writers during these years in China and particularly of their experiences as writers in relation to the Communist Party, see T.A. Hsia, *The Gate of Darkness,* Seattle 1968; Merle Goldman, *Literary Dissent in Communist China,* Cambridge 1967, or in paperback New York 1971; Jonathan Spence, *The Gate of Heavenly Peace,* New York 1981. See also my *Straw Sandals: Chinese Stories 1918-1933,* Cambridge 1974.

For a quick overview of events in China, especially during the last century, see Lucian W. Pye, *China: An Introduction,* 3rd edition, Boston 1984.

For a graphic picture of the Cultural Revolution as experienced by a Chinese student and members of his family, see Liang Heng and Judith Shapiro, *Son of the Revolution,* New York 1983.

For the interplay among different groups of intellectuals in this period, see Merle Goldman, *China's Intellectuals: Advise and Dissent,* Cambridge 1981.

ROMANIZATIONS

Modified Wade-Giles or other common usage	Pinyin
Ai Ching	Ai Qing
Chao Pu-chu	Zhou Puchu
Chen Han-seng	Chen Hansheng
Chen Kuo-fu	Chen Guofu
Chen Li-fu	Chen Lifu
Chen Ming	Chen Ming
Chen Shao-yu	Chen Shaoyu
Chen Tu-hsiu	Chen Duxiu
Chen Yi	Chen Yi
Chiang Ching	Jiang Qing
Chiang Ching-kuo	Jiang Jingguo
Chiang Kai-shek	—
Chu Chiu-pai	Qu Qiubai
Chou En-lai	Zhou Enlai
Chou Hai-en	Zhou Haien
Chou Yang	Zhou Yang
Chu Teh	Zhu De
Feng Keng	Feng Keng
Fong Mu	Fang Mu
Ho Chi Minh	—
Ho Meng-hsiung	Ho Mengxiong
Hsia Tsi-an	—
Hu Shih	Hu Shi
Hu Yao-pang	Hu Yaobang
Hua Kuo-feng	Hua Guofeng
Jou Shih	Rou Shi
Kang Sheng	Kang Sheng
Keng Chi-an	Geng Jian
Kuo Mo-jo	Guo Moruo
Ko Pao-chuan	Ge Baoquan
H. H. Kung	—
Li Shin	Li Xin
Li Wei-sen	Li Weisen
Lin Yu-tang	Lin Yutang

Liu Pin-yen	Liu Binyan
Liu Jen-ching	Liu Renqing
Liu Shao-chi	Liu Shaoqi
Liu Tsun-chi	Liu Zunqi
Lo Shih-yi	Lo Shiyi
Lo Teng-hsien	Lo Dengxian
Lu Hsun	Lu Xun
Ma Shin-yun	Ma Xinyun
Mao Tse-tung	Mao Zedong
Mao Tun	Mao Dun
Pan Tze-nien	Pan Zinian
Peng Teh-huai	Peng Dehuai
Soong Ai-ling	—
Soong Ching-ling	—
Soong Mei-ling	—
Soong, T.V.	—
Sun Yat-sen	—
Tang Tao	Tang Tao
Teng Hsiao-ping	Deng Xiaoping
Ting Ling	Ding Ling
Tong, Hollington	—
Tsai Ting-kai	Cai Tingkai
Tsai Yuan-pei	Cai Yuanbei
Tu Yueh-sheng	Du Yuesheng
Wang Chou-jan	Wang Zhouran
Wang, C.T.	—
Wang Hsin-ti	Wang Xindi
Wei Ching-sheng	Wei Jingsheng
Wu Chiang	Wu Qiang
Wu, Eugene	—
Yang Chien	Yang Jian
(Yang Hsin-fu)	(Yang Xinfu)
Yin Fu	Yin Fu
Ying Hsu-jen	Ying Xuren

Place Names

Anhwei	Anhui
Canton	Guangzhou
Changsha	Changsha
Chapei	Zhabei
Chekiang	Zhejiang
Chengtu	Chendu
Chien Men	Qianmen
Chingkang shan	Jinggangshan
Chungking	Chongqing
Dairen	Dalian
Foochow	Fuzhou
Hankow	Hangzhou

Heilungjiang	Heilongjiang
Honan	Henan
Hopeh	Hebei
Hunan	Hunan
Hongkew	Hongkou
Hungjao	Hongqiao
Ichang	Yichang
Jehol	Rehe
Kiangsi	Jiangxi
Kiangsu	Jiangsu
Kiukiang	Jiujiang
Kupeikow	Gubeikou
Luan River	Luan River
Lunghua	Longhua
Mukden	Shenyang
Nanking	Nanjing
Peking	Beijing
Peihai	Beihai
Pootoo	Putuo
Pootung	Pudong
Shanghai	Shanghai
Shansi	Shanxi
Shensi	Shaanxi
Sian	Sian
Soochow	Wusong

Suifu	Suifu
Szechwan	Sichuan
Tachienlu	Dajianlu
Taiwan	Taiwan
Tan Che-ssu	Tan Zhexu
Tibet	Xizang
Tienanmen	Tiananmen
Tientsin	Tianjin
Tsinghua	Qinghua
Tsaohoching	Zaohojing
Wanhsien	Wanxian
Whangpoo	Huangpu
Wuhan	Wuhan
Wo Fo-ssu	Wofosi
Woosung	Wusong
Wusih	Wuxi
Yangtze	Yangzi
Yenan	Yanan
Yunnan	Yunnan
Yuan Lung	Yuan Long

Other

Hsin Hua Yuei Pao	Xinhua yuebao
Kuomintang	Guomindang
Peida	Beida
Wen Yi Pao	Wenyi bao